Gold Start

Teaching Your Child About Money
Andrew Lendnal

16

EasyRead Large

RHYW

Copyright Page from the Original Book

First published 2011

Exisle Publishing Limited,
P.O. Box 60-490, Titirangi, Auckland 0642, New Zealand.
'Moonrising', Narone Creek Road, Wollombi, NSW 2325, Australia.
www.exislepublishing.com

National Library of New Zealand Cataloguing-in-Publication Data

Lendnal, Andrew, 1975-
Gold start: teaching your child about money / Andrew Lendnal.
Includes bibliographical references.
ISBN 978-1-877437-12-0
1. Children—Finance, Personal. 2. Parents—Finance, Personal.
332.0240083—dc 22

10 9 8 7 6 5 4 3 2 1

Text design and production by IslandBridge
Illustrations (pp. 64–5) by Mark Roman
Cover design by Christabella Designs
Printed in Singapore by KHL Printing Co Pte Ltd

This book uses paper sourced under ISO 14001 guidelines from
well-managed forests and other controlled sources.

TABLE OF CONTENTS

Also by Andrew Lendnal:

Budget Wise, Dollar Rich, with Anton Nadilo (Exisle Publishing)
Money Smart: children's picture book and audio book
Saving with Simon and Sue: children's picture book and audio book
The Camelot Way to Build and Protect your Financial Happiness

For more information on this book, visit:
www.goldstart.com.au or www.goldstart.co.nz

This book is dedicated with love to the memory of my late beloved mother.
Thank you for believing in me and always being there for me.

Parenting

par·ent [pair-uhnt, par-]

–noun

1. A father or a mother.

2. An ancestor, precursor or progenitor.

3. A source, origin or cause.

4. A protector or guardian.

5. Biology. Any organism that produces or generates another.

6. Physics. The first nuclide in a radioactive series.

–adjective

7. Being the original source: a parent organisation.

8. Biology. Pertaining to an organism, cell, or complex molecular structure that generates or produces another: parent cell; parent DNA.

–verb (used with object)

9. To be or act as parent of: to parent children with both love and discipline.

[Source: Dictionary.com, based on *The Random House Dictionary,* © Random House, Inc. 2010.]

I would like to add to this list: The hardest job in the world.

Of all the jobs in the world, being a parent is perhaps the most challenging. Our children are often hard to understand and difficult to control; finding the patience to cope can test the best of us. Sometimes, no matter how hard we try, it seems everything we do is wrong. No one can make parenting easy, but this book attempts to do its part by providing you with tools, information and activities to help with some of the challenges you may experience when it comes to teaching your children about money.

Introduction

Help me save my children from becoming victims of Generation Debt

You've done your best to raise loving, sensitive, talented, compassionate children. That's why you have picked up this book. They mean the world to you but, unfortunately, you feel you may not have done a great job of teaching them about money. And the last thing you want is to create further victims of Generation Debt – a term coined by author Anya Kamenetz (and the title of her first book).

Today's twenty-something generation tends to be made up of highly educated individuals who are often mired in unmanageable debt – credit cards, car and student loans. In Europe they're known as the '1000-Euro Generation', a moniker credited to an Italian internet novel. This generation doesn't understand a lot about money, but does like to spend it. The result can be tens of thousands of dollars in debt that won't go away.

It doesn't take long for the typical university student, persuaded on-campus to sign up for that first credit card, to max it out and sign up for a few more cards, using them to buy clothes and university course requirements.

When the debt catches up with these students, they take out student loans to pay it off and help make ends meet. By the time they leave university they're in a hole $20,000 deep. That doesn't stop them from taking out another ten (or 20) grand to buy a car.

A decade later, at 30, they're still chipping away at their $30,000 tab. Although they're saddled with debt and there's no end in sight, they're not losing any sleep over it. They find it hard to save and are frequently tempted by nice clothes and the latest technology. They see this penchant for living beyond their means as a mark of their generation, one made up of those who will drop $4 on a coffee without a second thought and who pride themselves on having the latest gadgets.

Our grandparents understood the value of a dollar. They stashed coins in piggy banks and contributed to their savings accounts. That was before credit cards, and when borrowing money to buy a car was out of the question. What happened to that old-fashioned virtue, thrift? We've taken the notion of living beyond our means to a whole new level, as we continue to live with debt and no savings.

Spending is no longer keeping up with the Joneses; now it's keeping up with the Hiltons.

(Matt Murray, executive director of the American Association of Young People)

Tertiary students may grow up with the illusion of a level playing field, but after they've finished their studies, there are those with $50,000 in loans and those without. This is a generation hugely divided. Unlike the baby-boomers, these young adults don't have a collective feeling. They face a series of economic and social issues their parents and grandparents never encountered. Sixty per cent of student aid is in the form of loans and the national average student loan in Australia is over A$22,000; in New Zealand it is nearly NZ$20,000. Taking out a student loan is now a rite of passage.

Credit cards, too, act as safety nets for tertiary students. Many give themselves an unwelcome graduation present – an average of $3000 in credit card debt at the time they receive a degree.

All this because we live in a financially illiterate culture where the financial crises of inexperienced spenders are regarded as simple mistakes! But there's no easy answer, no one-stop shop, crash diet or training regime to make you and your children fiscally fit.

We're not doing well with regard to money management. While some of the debt issues faced by younger generations can be addressed by more responsible money handling, a larger part of the problem lies in our ever-changing economy, and the urgent need for economic reform.

Learning the hard way

Here are some comments from parents, made with the benefit of hindsight.

I wish I'd made my son get a job

Let me start by saying that my son has been involved in sport since he was very young. What that means in regard to money management is that it's hard to work when you are constantly practising. I made a deal with him very early on that I would not give him any money; he would have to earn that himself. He did come up with a few entrepreneurial stints over the years, as a bush lawyer at high school and making custom CDs before the whole music downloading thing blew up. He once spent two weeks mowing lawns, which taught him the value of getting an education. For the most part, though, he didn't work. I wish I had made him get a regular job, even if it was only a few hours a week, because he would have acquired a work ethic.

My son is now in his final year of university and I've finally insisted. I asked him, at 21 with absolutely no work experience, who did he think would hire him when he graduated and was waiting to be picked up by a professional rugby team. It's going to take a top Japanese club a while to find him and, in the meantime, he will be competing for entry-level jobs with other 22-year-olds who've been working since they were 15 or 16.

So now he's working in his first regular job, as a delivery boy for Pizza Hut. What do you know? He likes working! He has learned about the anxiety of the first day on a new job and how that is survivable; he has learned about tax being deducted from his pay and, most of all, he has learned that he has to go to work in order to support his lifestyle – and because the other people who work there are counting on him. For these and lots of other reasons, I wish I had made my son get a job as soon as he was old enough to work.

I wish I'd insisted that my daughter save some of her money

When my daughter was small and doing occasional odd jobs, I did make her save some of her money. But I never set up a hard-and-fast rule about saving a certain percentage of her earnings. Now she doesn't have that habit and will have to figure it out on her own.

I wish I'd taught my son to budget

Along with not saving his money, my son doesn't know about budgeting. He is in his first year of flatting. I am paying half his rent and nothing else. Unlike the flat he had last year, he is also responsible for power bills. Last year he was forced to learn a little about budgeting when he had to start buying his own groceries. I know these are real-life lessons that we all learn at some point, but I wish I had better prepared him. On the brighter side, at least he is learning them now before he really gets out on his own!

I wish I'd insisted my daughter give a portion of her money to charity

I love the idea of giving a small child a dollar and then making her give some of it to someone who needs it more. I love the idea of taking my children to volunteer at the food bank or help out at the local SPCA. I never did any of that and I wish I had.

I wish I'd taught my son to manage his money

When my son was first going off to university I realised that, never having had a cheque account, he probably didn't really know how to use one. I was right! Before he left I sat him down and made him balance my cheque book. That was an experience for him. Among other things, he learned Mum *isn't* actually made of money! It was a good lesson for him but I wish I had started sooner. He duly opened a cheque account when he first went off to university. He no longer has one. I don't know why, but I suspect he got into some trouble with it and his debit card. Another lesson learned!

I wish I'd talked with my daughter about the dangers of credit cards

I don't know if she has a credit card. I know she is inundated with offers. If she does, her ability to manage it will not have come from anything I ever taught her because I don't believe we ever talked about it.

Do you pass the financially savvy parent test?

I was raised to believe that you don't talk about money, and I'm not sure if the financial bumps in my life would have been smoothed out at all if my parents had discussed money management with me. But I would have had a better understanding, at an earlier age, of how it all works.

So, after you've read about the regrets some parents have, are you ready to involve your children actively in day-to-day financial dealings? The purpose of this book is to help prevent your children getting to the point of major indebtedness by making them fluent in finance and providing you with the necessary tools to pass on the four basic principles of money management – earning, saving, spending and sharing.

It's important to teach money basics at an early age. Getting in front of the behaviour before it has a chance to set is the recipe for creating a society of financially literate adults.

Financially savvy parents know how to emphasise healthy, positive money behaviours that communicate strong values to their children. They also know how to minimise negative money behaviours that send the wrong messages. They are able to identify teachable times that help them talk to their children about money, answer their questions and teach them to reflect on financial decisions.

As a financially savvy parent, you understand that money is in itself neither good nor bad; it's what you do with it and what you teach your children about it that is important.

By answering the following questions correctly, either 'Yes' or 'No', you will find out if you are a financially savvy parent:

1. Do you have unresolved issues around money, i.e. do you spend too much, or do you have difficulty spending money at all? Have you made poor investments? Do you have difficulty saving money?

2. Do you have goals and a plan to educate your children about financial matters?

3. Do you think about the values you're communicating to your children through your money behaviours?

4. Are you uncomfortable talking about money with your children?

5. If your children ask for something you don't want to buy because you think it's too expensive, poorly made or they already have enough, do you take the time and effort to explain why you're saying no?

6. Do you sometimes use money as a bribe?

7. If you feel you've been too busy to spend time with your children, do you try to make it up to them by buying them things?

8. Do you and your spouse often argue about money in front of your children?

9. Do your children go to the other parent when they don't get an answer they want?

10. Do you ever talk to your children about the importance of charity and helping others less fortunate than your family? Do you help your children get involved in charitable activities?

11. Do you give your children a consistent allowance?

12. Do you think it's important to have a healthy relationship with money?

You may not have given much thought to the issues raised by this questionnaire; financially savvy parenting isn't an inbuilt skill. Our own parents' money issues, combined with societal attitudes, shape our money beliefs and behaviours, and they haven't always been shaped in ways that benefit our children.

If you gave the right answers to these questions, you're on your way to becoming a financially savvy parent. If you didn't, then the lessons outlined in this book are here to help you and your family. The correct answers are: 1. No; 2. Yes; 3. Yes; 4. No; 5. Yes; 6. No; 7. No; 8. No; 9. No; 10. Yes; 11. Yes; 12. Yes.

Rules of engagement – the war against debt

Here are some strategies that may help you win the battle:

- Speak with your spouse or partner first so that you'll both be on the same page when it's time to talk to the children about financial priorities.

- Put yourself in your children's shoes; try to remember what your top financial concerns and priorities were at that age.

- Next, ask them about their thoughts on money. It'll show you're interested in their opinion and help to make conversations about money more productive.

Everyone needs to understand about money: where it comes from, how to spend it wisely, how to save and invest for the future – and don't forget the principle of giving. Too many parents don't take the time to teach their children about the values of money and, unfortunately, many of those children grow up to be adults who struggle with basic money management skills.

The benefits of teaching children good money habits make it well worth the effort. Children who aren't taught these lessons suffer the consequences for a lifetime. Some parents don't teach children about money because they see it as a taboo subject, don't have the time or think they don't have enough money to make it worthwhile discussing. Parents should take the time to teach children about money regardless of income, and they should start when the children are young.

This process needs to begin preferably before children reach school age, and certainly before their teen years. This book contains some helpful guidelines and suggestions. It provides a general background and outlines by age-group and stage of development children's understanding and use of money, as well as conflicts about money. It also identifies activities you can use to teach your child about money.

Most people have strong feelings and opinions about money, based on childhood experiences and the values and beliefs of their families. Usually these experiences, values and beliefs differ between parents. It's vital for the healthy development of children that parents talk about these feelings and opinions, and establish a consistent approach to teaching children about money.

These questions can help you focus your discussion:

- How do we create an open environment to discuss money issues?

- How should our children receive money?

- What are our family values and attitudes about money?

- What should we tell our children about money?

- How should we use everyday examples to teach money skills?

- How will we deal with our children's differences in handling money?

- How will we respond to the effects of advertising and peer pressure on our children?

Keep these questions in mind as you begin socialising your children financially.

How do children learn about money?

Children learn about money from their parents. They watch their parents spend or save money every day (observation). They also hear their parents talk about money, either directly or indirectly (talking it over). And children learn about money by using it themselves (learning by doing).

Observation

Children see what their parents and other adults do with money and they start to understand how their parents feel about it. In turn, this influences their own feelings about money. Do the parents spend all their money before it's earned? If so, this may make it hard to teach children about limited resources, planning for spending and the value of saving. Or do the parents save every cent they earn? This may make it hard for children to see that money is a tool, not a goal in and of itself, and can make it difficult for children to spend even for necessities.

Talking it over

It is important to discuss the family's financial situation with children at a level appropriate for their age. Encourage children to participate in family financial discussions. Communicate about money one-on-one as the opportunity comes up. For example, your daughter wants to buy a digital camera. You tell her that you can't afford it. Then the next week you buy a new car. What does your daughter think? Help her understand why it's important to have the car to drive to work and why that need must come before buying her a digital camera.

When talking about money and saving with children, encourage them to set realistic goals for the near future. Saving money for that new digital camera is more realistic than saving for retirement at the daughter's age. Remember children live in the present.

Also, be reassuring when talking to children about money. If they discover the house they live in is not completely paid for, they may worry. Assure them the family is able to make the monthly payments and they won't be out in the street by morning.

Learning by doing

The best way children learn is by doing. This book provides you with numerous useful tools and activities to reinforce the lessons you are about to learn on your journey to becoming a financially savvy parent. Choose the activities that are appropriate for the child's age and current interests.

Remember, money gives people – both young and old – decision-making opportunities. Educating, motivating and empowering children to become regular savers and investors will enable them to keep more of the money they earn, and to do more with the money they spend. Everyday spending decisions can have a far more negative impact on children's financial futures than any investment decisions they may ever make. To ensure that your children will be financially literate adults, you are about to be introduced to 15 simple lessons you'll wish your parents and teachers had taught you about money when you were young.

Lesson 1

The sooner you start, the less scary it will be

Start early to raise financially responsible adults

When your child is old enough to start asking, 'Buy me this' or 'Buy me that', it's time to start talking to them about money. Up till now they didn't ask, and you bought them what they needed. Now they're starting to express wants and needs of their own. We all want to give our children the best, but how do we draw a line under what they should ask for, and what they should get?

Before children start asking for things they're not ready to understand the concept of money. But once they have personal wants – a toy, some McDonald's, new clothes or wanting you to take them somewhere that costs money – it's time to start talking to them about money. The first thing you need to discuss with them is that things are not free, that when you buy them something, or take them where there's an entry fee, it costs money.

The benefits of teaching your children about money early on are both immediate and long term. In the short term you'll help them develop saving habits, learn how to make smart purchases, begin to understand the meaning of 'investment' and perhaps even learn why they can't have everything they want straight away. In the long term, you can help them avoid accumulating debt. And by teaching the value of saving for the future you can help them plan for financial security.

If you can show a young child what to do with her money as soon as she knows what money is, she'll develop habits that will serve her well throughout her life. This is the first step to learning how to earn, save, spend and share effectively.

We must help our children learn to compartmentalise, i.e. to manage money. Otherwise, they'll get into the habit of regarding their allowance as a licence to buy movie tickets, toys, music and clothes. That's not a realistic view. As adults, if they treat their pay the way they've treated their allowance, they'll be in real trouble.

As soon as your children can count, or grasp the transaction involved in buying sweets, they're ready for an explanation about money. Whatever their age, you can help your children both by giving advice, direct and indirect, and by setting a good example. Let them use money. Provide opportunities to start using money early on, but give them small amounts so their mistakes won't be too costly.

What they should know and when

To ensure your children are on-track, you need to be aware of the stages at which each child's financial growth takes place. Remember, children are unique individuals who develop at their own rate but all of them, as they grow older, must be included to an ever greater extent in discussions of limits and consequences.

Age Group	Skills Used/Learned
Infants and toddlers	• Language skills
	• Different items
Preschool	• Exchanging
	• Touch and feel
School-age	• Addition
	• Sorting
	• Combining different money values

Three to five: it's never too early to turn them into junior tycoons

I don't really recommend that you get serious with your toddler about the share market, but there are some simple games you can play that will entertain your child while building a basic understanding of money. For example:

• Try playing shopkeeper. Have your child price items with coloured stickers and use play-money to buy them. Keep the sales revenue in a bank. Switch roles – shopkeeper and shopper – with your child.

- Let your children handle supermarket coupons, matching them with the appropriate items (let them keep the savings). Explain your choices as you shop – how sale items are cheaper, and why bigger sizes are a better deal.

- Talk to them about coins and notes, and help them start to understand that the different sizes are worth different amounts. Then offer to trade them your 10-cent coins for their 50-cent coins.

Six to eight: it's allowance time

It's a good idea to give your children a monthly allowance (monthly so they have to plan ahead). At this age, children can begin to estimate the cost of purchases and figure out how to get correct change.

Test them by handing them some money and letting them count it. Or let them pay for the burgers and fries. If they bring back the correct change, let them keep it (assuming you didn't give them a fifty). Teach them about value by letting them buy a bargain brand of juice, then compare the taste with the brand they're used to. Don't forget to point out the money they saved. Make a game of looking at price tags for markdowns and sale items.

Setting limits

We all have to live within our means. One way to instil some discipline about spending is to set a limit on what you're willing to spend on clothing (or other common expenses). If your children want something more expensive, they have to make up the difference.

Nine to 12: big eyes, small wallets

At this age, it's appropriate for your children to start earning extra money in order to supplement their allowance. And some pre-teens develop an interest in investing. Hey, you could be raising the next Bill Gates. If so, encourage that interest. Children this age also start to want a lot of stuff. So the next time your child says, 'Why can't I buy it?' try this. Count out your pay in cash. Separate the notes into stacks that represent food, rent, power, savings etc. Show your child in graphic detail why you're not made of money.

Borrowing may start to become an issue. Go ahead. Lend your child money, but make a point of charging interest. Finding out how much it costs to borrow money is an important lesson to learn. At the very least, have your child do odd jobs around the house to pay off the loan.

There are several more things you can do to help your pre-teen learn about money and its value in the world:

- Set short-term goals and save toward them.

- Make deposits in a savings account. Don't bother teaching them how to withdraw the money. That's usually an inherited trait.

- Show them how to comparison shop, and wait for sales.

- Set long-term goals so they experience the thrill of actually achieving those goals (you might learn something too).

Show them the money!
You can use money to teach:

Maths skills   Using money involves using different maths skills like adding, subtracting, matching and sorting. A child will learn how money 'works', and how best to use it in stages, depending on age and experience. As a parent, you can help your child learn to use money and develop useful skills.

Saving habits   Saving is an important part of learning how to manage money. Many children learn about saving by having piggy banks. Saving money can help children learn how to plan, develop patience and learn how to delay gratification. So whether you give your child an allowance, or money for doing something in particular, this is a good way to work with him on saving.

Making choices   Using money involves making choices. You start with a certain amount of money and you make choices on how to spend it. When shopping, let your child observe how you make choices. Explain briefly why you decided on brand A versus brand B. 'I could either buy this soap which smells good, or buy these two soaps which are on sale and will save me money.'

Allow your child to choose items sometimes when you are out shopping together. Offer a choice of two items that you find acceptable, and then allow her to choose one of them.

Community skills   Saving and sharing money can be used as part of a lesson in reaching a shared goal. It is also a good way to promote working with others. For example, allow your child to share in helping with a favourite charity, a family activity, or a community project. Allow an older child to help decide what kind of charity or project you want to work on as a family. If money is needed for the project, let your child contribute and decide how that money is to be used.

Social skills   Using money involves many social skills and interactions with others. From speaking with salespeople to the social rules that go with making a purchase, practising social skills is part of using money in everyday life.

Research has shown that a child with positive social skills is more likely to succeed in school and in life. Some children need a lot of help to develop these skills. Research also shows that a

8

child who isn't able to interact positively with others tends to be unable to make and keep friends, and may have behavioural problems at school.

Talking with your children at an early age about money and saving is important. You can help them form positive lifelong skills around money. This also involves learning and using other important life skills as well.

No matter what your financial circumstances or personal beliefs, you can help your child become 'money-smart' and learn to use the money system to his or her advantage.

Age Group	Skills Used/Learned
Infants and toddlers	• Observing the social interactions in making a purchase
	• Observing making choices
	• Pretending
Preschool	• Making choices
	• Learning money values
	• Getting ready for social interactions
School-age	• Practising roles in social interactions
	• Using practical math skills

What about tweens (12 to 14)?

School-age children eventually grow into high-school or college students, and the roller coaster of emotions, intellectual growth and social pitfalls gets faster, steeper and harder to predict. Children in high school are generally becoming more irritable, and mood swings are normal. Children are transitioning from a relatively sheltered life with few worries and responsibilities to the realisation that in a few short years they, too, will become part of the world that Mum and Dad inhabit. That world comes with a load of fears, failures and far-reaching consequences.

The young adolescent mix of childlike innocence and uncooperative stubbornness makes it hard to parent them, but this is the time they need parents the most. Peer pressure is at its most intense, and children's need for sound, consistent education in the managing of money and finances is greater than ever.

Skills Used/Learned

• Want to make earning and spending decisions without consulting parents

• May be dissatisfied with household income and what it provides

• May borrow from friends to satisfy money needs

• May ask to use parents' credit cards if their peers are doing so

- Can begin to earn and save for long-term goals

- Understand that planning allows the family to set financial goals and work together to reach them

- Begin to deal with abstract concepts

- Begin to set goals and make plans to reach goals

- Understand the trade-offs and consequences of their money management decisions

- Still need help in establishing limits

- Often test values with others

- Can see things from the viewpoint of others

...and teens?

When they reach their teens, children get serious about independence. They want to do what they want to do, and they'd appreciate it if you'd leave them alone. But they are also perfectly willing to spend your money – as long as you don't ask them what they're buying. What is a parent to do? This subject is covered in greater depth in a separate chapter ('Teens and money').

Teenagers, and the young adults they will soon become, worry a great deal about their peer relationships and how they are viewed within their group. They engage in power plays, make unwise decisions and sometimes change their physical appearance to the point that many a mother has been known to wring her hands in panic and frustration.

No matter what changes your teenager goes through, this is not the time to berate them for their choices or, even worse, compare them unfavourably with the model teen down the street. Instead, continue to be an example, to be available, and to transition into the role of friend. Very soon teenagers will leave home and need to be capable of standing on their own two feet; hence their personal leadership and team-building skills must have been developed. In addition, this will be the test of your success in educating them in financial matters...

Skills Used/Learned

- Desire independence, but often financially dependent

- May make impossible financial demands, often because of insecurities

- Their school, social life and activities are costly

- Peers often have more influence than parents

- Need to have money to manage

- May want to use credit for a major purchase

- Need to experience the good and bad consequences of spending actions

- Often continue to need help distinguishing wants and needs when making purchasing decisions

- Understand they can substitute time and energy for money, i.e., performing a task for someone in lieu of a purchased gift

- Understand differences between gross and net income and the importance of employment benefits

Family activity idea 1.1

Everyday money activities

There are many activities that can teach your children about money. Here are some suggestions for your preschoolers, school-age children and teenagers.

Preschoolers

• Play supermarket or bank with pretend money.

• Let them borrow or rent something they need to return.

• Have children do unpaid chores, like setting the table or putting away toys.

• Read stories about money.

School-age children

• Teach children to check prices in newspapers and circulars before buying.

• Help establish the amount of their earnings to be saved, and why.

• Play Monopoly or Pay Day games.

• Plan how to share the cost of an item they cannot afford from their earnings.

Teenagers

• Open a cheque account and help them balance it.

- Help them understand the use of cash and credit.

- Help children return an item or write a letter of complaint about an unsatisfactory item.

- Allow participation in family financial discussions about what to buy, how to save more, and how to cut expenses.

Lesson 2

The value of values

Pass them on

Money doesn't grow on trees. It sprouts from an automatic teller machine. From your children's perspective it does, anyway. Mum pushes a few magic buttons and money appears. Why would they think there are limits?

Values stand behind everything we do. Values tell us what the good life is. Values shape our ambitions for what we want our lives to be. We show our values in the way we talk and act, in how we spend our time and effort, in our actions at work and leisure and in our spending choices.

Knowing what is important to us helps us understand ourselves better. Knowing our children's values makes it easier to understand them and why they do things as they do. As individuals, we all have different values and attitudes toward spending and saving money. This is part of what makes each of us unique. When the values of family members differ, there is potential conflict.

If we determine what is important to us and why, our values become clear. These values influence how we spend our money. Values also influence how we save for important things. The following exercise might help you decide what your values are:

Work Are you satisfied with your job? Do you make as much money as you would like? How do you feel about both husband and wife working outside the home? Are you willing to move for job advancement? Are you willing to move for your spouse's job advancement?

Home Do you want to rent or own a home? Can you afford to furnish your own home as you would like?

Transportation Could you get along without a car? Could your family get along with one car? Would you be willing to drive less? Would you join a car pool? Would you be satisfied with a smaller car?

Recreation What do you do for recreation? Would you be satisfied spending less money on recreation or hobbies?

Future security Are you comfortable buying now and paying later? How important is saving? Have you started to plan for retirement? How would you provide for your family in case of death or disability?

Unrealistic values

Financial disaster is sometimes the result of wanting more than you can afford. Young families often have money problems because they expect to have immediately the things that took their parents years to achieve. Social pressure may lead families into buying a car, a home or expensive furnishings. Media advertising encourages us to overspend. For all of these reasons, families may find themselves with money problems.

Peer pressure

Your child wants a pair of Nike shoes; you think she or he will do just fine with the store brand of shoe. The compromise is clear: you are willing to contribute the amount of money that the store brand costs, and leave it up to your child to earn the difference. What may not be so obvious is the learning experience. Your child will now understand that she can have everything her friends have, but she is expected to help make this happen. Your child will learn that some things may not be worth the effort, while others are. Additionally, your child has far more stock in the investment than her friends, and will probably be more careful with it.

Peer pressure refers to how others your children's age can influence their thinking, intentionally or otherwise. Peer pressure is one of the strongest influences on young people. Friends, classmates, teammates and workmates are usually very important to them. At the same time, all these young people are in a similar situation – trying to figure out their lives, experimenting, trying to decide what they truly value.

Many of the decisions young people make will be influenced by their peers. Situations can arise that involve making decisions related to alcohol, smoking, drugs, clothing fads and styles, concerts, schools, careers, jobs and so on. Many of these are difficult decisions, and peers can apply a great deal of pressure – either directly, or by the decisions they've made and the actions they're taking. There will be times when values are really put to the test.

As far as money matters go, your children's peers may seek to influence them – how much they spend, what they buy, how much they borrow, what styles they follow. Once again, it's important your children know how to make decisions that they believe are best for them, the ones that fit their values, priorities and goals.

Fortunately, most nine- to 12-year-olds still talk about money with their parents and understand several basic financial concepts. For instance, most children in this age group know what a debt is, or at least understand the general concept. But very few children this age know how much it really costs to keep a family going for a week. The concepts of income and expenses are still fuzzy at this age, although children understand that their parents need money to buy things.

Keeping up with the Joneses

There are any number of reasons why some people have more than others – generous parents, an inheritance, a good job, trading off other things, effective saving, hard work or a large debt. Children need to learn to make good judgements about trying to keep up with, or get ahead of, others.

Advertising

The advertising industry seeks to sway us, and our children, to value certain goods above others. Ask your children to 'advertise' some item in their room as if they were putting it on TradeMe; chances are they will embellish the truth a bit and fail to mention the scuff marks. Explain that media advertising works the same way, that ads create needs that only the advertised product can, supposedly, fill. Your child should be able to recognise that advertisements are sneaky ways of manipulation, even if a revered sporting hero is hocking the item.

Generally speaking, children between the ages of nine and 12 develop consumption habits that will stay with them for the rest of their lives. On the other hand, they can also learn a lot from their mistakes. Many already have a bank account in their own name, the money coming perhaps from birthday gifts, rewards from parents or grandparents, weekly allowances or payment for odd jobs.

Nine- to 12-year-olds have a surprising amount of purchasing power – both with their own money and through their influence on the spending habits of their parents and other adults. This, along with the fact that children this age tend to spend their money quickly and impulsively, is why they are targeted by advertisers.

Value conflicts

Each of us has our own set of values. When there are differences in values within the family, you must try to agree on common goals. Talking about money is not always easy. The more open your family is about money talk, however, the more satisfied all will be with how family money is spent.

Family involvement

In some families, one person makes all the decisions about money. This person is often the breadwinner. Families that believe whoever earns the money should decide how it's spent often have problems sticking to a spending plan.

If both partners work together to make money decisions, there are fewer arguments. If parents talk openly with their children about finances, the children are usually more willing to carry out decisions.

Breaking the ice

Keep these guidelines in mind when you talk with your family about money, and be honest about your financial situation.

- Remember that each family member will have different values and goals.

- Acknowledge that conflict may arise. Don't avoid it.

- Learn to manage conflict. Respect family members' differences. Work toward a decision agreeable to all.

- State your wants, needs, feelings and thoughts.

- Allow family members to do the same.

- Allow time. Don't rush the person talking.

- Use I-messages (I think..., I feel...). Avoid you-messages (You always..., I feel like you never...). I-messages state your own reactions. You-messages blame the other person and say, I'm right.

Listen to one another. Tell each other how you feel and what you think of what others are saying. Be sure you understand what others say: repeat, but in your own words, what you think the other person is trying to say. Be flexible. If necessary, compromise your own desires for the good of the family.

Involving children

Children learn about money by watching their parents. They also learn by practising money management. Children who take part in regular discussions about using the family income learn how to make decisions. Children influence the family's spending even if they don't earn money. The wants and needs of children are part of the family budget.

The emotional power of money

Money is powerful. It can bring out the best and worst in people, so understanding money's influence can help a family gain control over their finances. Insight into the emotional power of money can help prepare a family to handle sensitive issues when they arise. Some emotional aspects of money are positive: security, comfort, freedom, sharing and so on. Others can work against a family.

Answer the following True (T)/False (F) questions about your use of money. Be honest!

1. I buy things I don't want or need because they are on sale.	T	F
2. I feel anxious and defensive when asked about my personal finances.	T	F
3. I can never have enough money saved to feel secure.	T	F
4. I buy things I don't need or want because they are fashionable.	T	F
5. I overspend regularly on extras.	T	F

6. I often insist on paying more than my share at a restaurant or on a group gift.	T	F
7. I spend money freely, even foolishly, on others but seldom on myself.	T	F
8. I feel dumb if I pay more for something than a neighbour did.	T	F
9. I don't trust others in my family to spend money wisely.	T	F
10. If I earn money, I think I should have the right to decide how it is spent.	T	F
11. If someone in my family acts selfishly in spending our money on him/herself, I feel I have the right to do the same.	T	F

Adapted from Family Communications about Money by Cindy Darden and Mary Jane Shumard, Cooperative Extension Service, The University of Georgia College of Agriculture, September 1985.

If you answered *True* to any of questions 1–3, you may feel insecure concerning money. Money is a form of security, but not the only one. What other aspects of life might be causing your feeling of insecurity? Think about it.

Did you answer *True* to either 4 or 5? Perhaps you see money as a way of gaining status. Money sometimes reflects the values of others, rather than our own.

True answers to questions 6, 7 or 8 might mean you use money to boost your self-esteem. Spending on others does not win the affection of family members, friends or co-workers. Your spending is your business and has nothing to do with the spending of your neighbours. You can't buy self-esteem. If yours is low, seek help through reading, therapy, changes in appearance or actions, but not through money.

If you answered *True* to questions 9 and/or 10, you may be using money to control others in the family. In double-income families, his/her money divisions can cause resentment. Not involving family members often results in lack of co-operation. A dictator may secure obedience, but not love. Which do you want from your family?

A *True* answer to question 11 may indicate that money is used for retaliation, to get back at someone. Fairness can become such an issue it blocks love and affection. If you need to disagree, do so without using money as your weapon.

When emotional uses of money go unrecognised, trouble brews. Try to prevent it.

Family council meetings

One way to get everybody involved in money decisions is by holding family council meetings. These meetings help each member explore their own beliefs, values and wishes. They also offer the chance to voice complaints, ask questions and make suggestions. The family council meeting is the time for formulating plans and making decisions.

MoneyTalk activity

The following MoneyTalk activity may be used to help your family start a discussion on the values of money. This activity will help identify values and set financial goals. Each capable member should complete the following worksheet separately. Be specific and honest with your answers. As a parent you will need to define some of the terms for your school-aged children.

After completing the worksheet, compare your answers. Discuss how you agree or disagree. Are you able to pinpoint the conflicts?

Family activity idea 2.1

MoneyTalk Worksheet

Directions Family members should answer these questions separately, then compare answers. The similarities and differences that turn up can spark a discussion of family money attitudes, values and practices.

1 If you received $1000 tax-free, what would you do with it?

$ _____ for_____

$ _____ for_____

$ _____ for_____

$ _____ for_____

$ _____ for_____

$ _____ for_____

2 Rank the following activities. Use 1 to indicate what you would enjoy doing the most and 6 to indicate what you would enjoy least.

_____ An evening at home with the family

_____ A night on the town

_____ A few extra hours on the job

_____ Some quiet time to myself

_____ Spending time with friends

_____ Involvement in physical activity

3 If you had to make a major cut in your current spending, what area would you cut first?

[Space left intentionally blank in original book]

4 Do you agree or disagree with the following statements?

I'm basically too tight with money.	A	D
My spouse/parents is/are basically too tight with money.	A	D
Equality in family decision-making is important to me.	A	D
I feel good about the way financial decisions are made in my family.	A	D
Sometimes I buy things I don't need just because they're on sale.	A	D
I believe in enjoying today and letting tomorrow take care of itself.	A	D

5 I'd like to see us spend less money on

[Space left intentionally blank in original book]

and see more dollars go towards

[Space left intentionally blank in original book]

6 Which money problem is the most frequent cause of argument?

[Space left intentionally blank in original book]

28

7 What was the most sensible thing you've done in your family with money?

[Space left intentionally blank in original book]

And the most foolish?

[Space left intentionally blank in original book]

8 Can you fill in the following blank spaces for your household?

Family take-home income $ _____

Rent or mortgage payment $ _____

Money spent on food each month $ _____

Monthly car payment $ _____

9 Monthly credit card and HP payments amount to?

[Space left intentionally blank in original book]

Family activity idea 2.2

Think about your responsibility to others

Describe a hypothetical or real-life situation that highlights how people depend on your children and expect to get value for the money they pay them.

Here's an example:

You walk your neighbour's dog after school. Your neighbour counts on you to do the job. She gives you $10 a week. However, you lose interest after a month and stop walking the dog. What are the consequences?

There are many individuals, groups and situations that can influence your children's values, some actively and others without even trying. Exercise caution with those who set out to influence what your children do and the decisions they make.

Lesson 3

Breaking the materialism trap

The difference between needs, wants and wishes

We need to teach children about consumerism, the excesses of materialism and the dangers of advertising. We need to show them that not everything of value comes via the cash register. So what should parents and guardians do?

- Teach your children the value of money, and that not everything that looks good is in fact desirable.

- Teach children to distinguish between needs and wants.

- Don't allow your children to pester you. They may whine, beg, cry, shout and do you favours to get what they want, but ask them if their survival really depends on whether or not they get it.

- Teach them discernment – why fruit makes a healthier snack than sugar- and salt-laden junk food is a good start.

- One more thing: they should also see that you as parents practise what you preach. If you start with this, the rest will be that much easier.

Wishing versus needing

Teaching children the difference between what they want and what they actually need could well be every bit as important as making sure they get good grades.

Needs vary from person to person, but there are some things we all must have to survive: food, air, water, clothing and shelter. Wishes on the other hand express our desires, and while it's normal to wish for things children need to understand that not all wishes can be granted. Explain that wishes are less important than needs. Compare what your child wishes for with a basic need, like food.

Wishes are more specific than needs and usually quite personal. But the distinction can become blurred because people can meet the same basic needs by fulfilling different wishes. Children between the ages of nine and 12 can have difficulty grasping the difference between the two concepts.

Recognising wishes masquerading as needs

Advertising promotes wishes over needs. Help your child understand that basic needs like food, clothing and shelter transform into wishes when they become more specific. For example, a child might want a particular brand of clothing. The garment satisfies the need to keep warm, but the brand is influenced by a wish.

Although there are only a few basic needs, wishes are limitless. Unsatisfied wishes don't have an impact on health and comfort the way unsatisfied needs do. Children must understand the difference because they make their own consumption choices, and influence yours as well.

Children who understand the difference between wants and needs are:

- more likely to save for what they want instead of using credit

- less likely to be swayed by emotive marketing techniques

- less likely to throw a tantrum in the supermarket

- less likely to judge their own worth by what they own.

But teaching your children the difference between wants and needs isn't something you can do in one easy lesson. It's an ongoing process, one that you can begin by laying down one simple ground rule for your child:

I will always, always take care of your needs. You will never go without food, clothes, shelter or school supplies. I am not here to

give you everything you'll ever want. But I love you very much, and if there is something you want, I will show you how to save for it – just like I do.

This statement will cover most situations when a child of any age is begging for something that they want, but do not need.

Let's also take a look at a few specific examples that will provide you with further opportunities to teach your child the difference between wants and needs.

Buying school stationery
Children need school supplies in order to complete their education and have a good experience at school. And school supplies can be expensive.

If your child is old enough, you can hand her the list of supplies she needs and an amount of cash you're comfortable spending. Help her then keep track of the cost of the items in the shopping cart, and ask her to tick the items off the list as she decides what she wants.

Now, the beauty of this plan is that your child will mess up. At first she will probably pick out the most expensive calculator, pens and so on. Use your cellphone calculator and keep a running total. Use the experience as a chance to talk about the real value of the items she is buying. Yes, she needs a hardcover notebook. But can she afford to spend $8 on a single notebook?

Do be careful not to assign the value *for* your child. The whole point is for her to figure it out on her own while you're there to support her. Yes, obviously a 50-cent notebook is more affordable. But your child may attach great value to the $8 one. This is the perfect time for you to help her question why she wants it:

- Is it a better notebook? Higher quality?

- Do they have any other notebooks like it at home?

- Does it have a cool picture on the front?

- Is it a cooler notebook than her friends will have?

If you can show her she'll have to sacrifice in other areas if she wants the more expensive item, that's a valuable lesson too. Just make sure you don't give your child additional money to buy what she wants – that will defeat the purpose.

Letting your child pick her own school supplies can be an excellent experience for both of you – if you can let her go and allow her to make mistakes right there in the store. It also requires a fair amount of patience, not to mention moving things in and out of the shopping trolley. If she manages to get everything she needs and stay within budget, make sure you celebrate a bit. Tell her you're proud of her and buy a treat, or better still schedule some family time together.

At the supermarket

Taking your child to the supermarket gives you a wonderful opportunity to teach her about marketing. It can be frustrating when she wants every sugar-coated cereal and soft drink she's seen advertised on TV.

You can try all of the following:

- Ask her about the ad. Why did she like it? Why did it make her want the product? Does she think her life will become like that depicted in the commercial if you buy the product?

- Show her the price difference between the item she wants and another, less expensive, quality item.

- Before you leave the house allow her to add a single 'want' item to the shopping list. Talk to her about impulse buying. If she sees something else she wants, tell her she has to wait until next week and think about the purchase.

- Make her use her own money to buy the item. Few things drive the point home better than having to decide whether or not to spend your own cash on a purchase.

No matter how you go about teaching your children about wants and needs, they will benefit from it. Don't worry if you make a mistake, or give in once in a while. Smart purchasing and money management skills are learnt over a lifetime. Don't be afraid to get in there and lay the groundwork for your child. However you do it, it will make a firm foundation.

Family activity idea 3.1

Distinguish between needs and wishes

Use these examples (or others more specific to your family) to show your child the difference between basic needs and wishes. Ask him to identify which are needs and which are wants.

- a designer shirt
- clothing
- a new jacket from Store X
- food
- their favourite XBox game
- a music CD
- a meal at a fast-food restaurant
- a telephone
- their uncle's luxury car
- transportation
- a new house in an expensive suburb
- a home.

The following questions will provoke further discussion:

1 Which of the needs listed above are crucial for a family's survival, and why?

2 Which needs are linked to wishes?

3 Can you name household items that enable you to meet specific needs?

4 Can you name household items that enable you to fulfil specific wishes?

Family activity idea 3.2

Give it up

Try the following activity to help your child understand that people must make choices and that, when people choose, they give something up.

1 The next time you're out shopping with your child (or visit a shopping website with her), make sure you have a piece of paper and pencil. Swing through the toy department (or books, clothes or wherever your child will have significant wants). Make a list with your child of five items she wants to buy, each costing $5 or less. Take the list home.

2 At home sit down with your child and ask her to rank the five items with number 1 being the item most wanted. Encourage your child to think of good and bad points about each item.

3 After you've completed the ranking, circle the top two. Suppose your daughter's first choice is a yo-yo and her second is a T-shirt, then she 'gives up' the yo-yo.

4 Ask your child to draw a picture of the two items, to circle the picture of the item she would buy and to put an 'X' through the picture of the item she's giving up.

5 Emphasise the idea that spending choices ALWAYS involve giving up something.

Scoring

If you completed this activity with your child pretty much as suggested, AND you purchased none of the items, give yourself five points.

If you completed this activity, but went back and purchased the number 1 item on the list, give yourself two points.

If you bought all five items before leaving the store and completing the activity, give yourself minus five points!

Lesson 4

Ready, set goals!

The fundamentals of ensuring your children's future

Teaching children to set and achieve goals is a huge responsibility. The ability to determine one's goals is a necessity for living a fulfilling life. Those who fail to learn how to set goals and work towards achieving them find themselves floundering about, constantly searching for answers.

Having a goal gives you a target to shoot for. Without a target, you can never hit a bull's-eye.

Goal-setting

The ability to set goals is something that needs to be taught. It doesn't come naturally to most people. Although life lessons can be a valuable teacher as well, these may not in themselves be enough to teach the importance of goals. Therefore, it's the job of parents, guardians, teachers, coaches and anyone else working with children to help them understand the need to set goals. They must also learn how to set goals, how to work toward them and how to monitor their own success.

Teaching children why to set goals

The importance of goal-setting is an abstract concept for children. Make it as concrete as possible with an analogy. Ask children to plan as a group what they're going to take with them on holiday. Inevitably, they will come to the conclusion that they first need to know where they are going. Do they need summer or winter clothes? Do they need a lot of clothing or a little? Do they need to pack food? Do they need hiking shoes? Without knowing their destination, they can't make plans.

At this point children begin to understand the need to have a goal in mind. Without a goal, how can they decide on a course of action?

Teaching children how to set goals

The next step is to teach children how to set their goals. This can be tricky; some children will feel overwhelmed. Remind them that goals don't have to be big decisions, such as what they want to be when they grow up. Also it's okay for goals to change.

Have children focus on short-term goals, such as completing all their assignments on time for the year, taking the rubbish out without being reminded, or obtaining a certain position in a rugby or netball team.

Setting S.M.A.R.T. goals

Specific A goal must be specific. A goal is specific if it can be clearly stated in one or two sentences. It should clearly detail what you want to achieve.

Measurable A goal must have a specific outcome to be achieved. For a goal to be effective you need to be able to measure whether it has been achieved, or not. The more detailed a goal is, the more likely it is to be measurable.

Acceptable A goal is acceptable if it fits with your values and is something you truly want. The thought of achieving your goal should be exciting.

Realistic A worthy goal should challenge you, but it also needs to be realistic. Analyse your strengths and weaknesses. Do you think you could achieve it?

Time frame Don't forget to include a time frame to achieve your goal. Setting a date means you can put a plan in place to achieve it.

Teaching children to write down their goals

Goals MUST be written down. People who claim to have it all in their head are kidding themselves. Writing down your goals serves to cement them in your mind, and makes you accountable for achieving them. This is a powerful motivator for many people.

A great tool for your children is a savings goal sheet (see section entitled "Teaching children how to monitor their success"). Get them to draw pictures of their goals (they can find photos on the internet or in a magazine) and describe them, then stick their goal sheet on a wall where they can see it every day.

Teaching children how to work toward their goals

Once a child has a goal in mind, he will need to be shown how to work towards it. Many children do set goals for themselves, but these are often unrealistic or go unmet because the child lacks the skills to achieve them.

Help your children to break down the steps necessary to reach their goals. For example, the child wanting to complete projects on time can come up with a plan to work on them every day immediately after school. The child who wants to gain a certain position in a sports team may plan to practise for a certain amount of time every day.

Individual circumstances will differ according to each child's goal. But the more you can help children break down the steps to achieving it, the more likely the child will be to succeed in reaching the goal.

Teaching children how to monitor their success

Children often have a tendency to give up when they hit a roadblock. You need to teach them how to monitor their own success and to judge honestly whether steps are being made in the right direction. Remind children they have already created their map; they need to check that map now and again to make sure they're still on the right track. And let them know it's okay to change the route now and again. That's the great thing about maps – there's more than one road to the same destination! (See 'Goal tracker')

45

Savings goal worksheet

I'm saving for the next .... months for the following goal(s):

Draw or stick pictures
of your goal(s) here

A description of my goal(s):

My goal(s) will cost: $ ....

46

Goal tracker

Use one goal-tracking sheet per savings goal to keep track of your progress towards achieving that goal. Enter all deposits you make, plus any withdrawals.

My goal: .... Date: ....

Description	Deposit	Withdrawal	Balance

First-time goal-setters

The last week of the year is when people typically start to evaluate what they did that year and set some goals for the following one. But many parents forget to include their children in this powerful process. Children of almost any age can be included in your goal-setting process, while helping them set a few of their own. And if you've never set goals before, this is the perfect time to start.

The big difference between successful and unsuccessful people is that the former group write their goals down on paper, AND they write them down on a regular basis. How hard is that?

If that's the deciding factor in whether or not a person is successful (that and a bit of action!), then setting and achieving goals has to be one of the many life skills you should be modelling for your children.

If you've never really sat down long enough to consider where you're going or what you want in life, that's okay – you can start now. The past is the past; let it go. The future, however, is like a brand-new sketch book ready for your creations.

Oh, you thought you had to WRITE your goals? Well, that's a great start but you can also create something called a Dream (or Vision) Board. Napoleon Hill, the author of *Think and Grow Rich,* once said, 'What the mind can conceive and believe, the mind can achieve.'

48

Great quote! We need to teach our children this concept early in life!

Creating a Dream (or Vision) Board

This is a simple, fun process but it will take some thought and a focus on the question: What do I want in life? Before you begin building your Dream Board, write this question at the top of a piece of paper, sit down quietly and answer it. Have each child who is creating a board with you do the same. Children generally love this part!

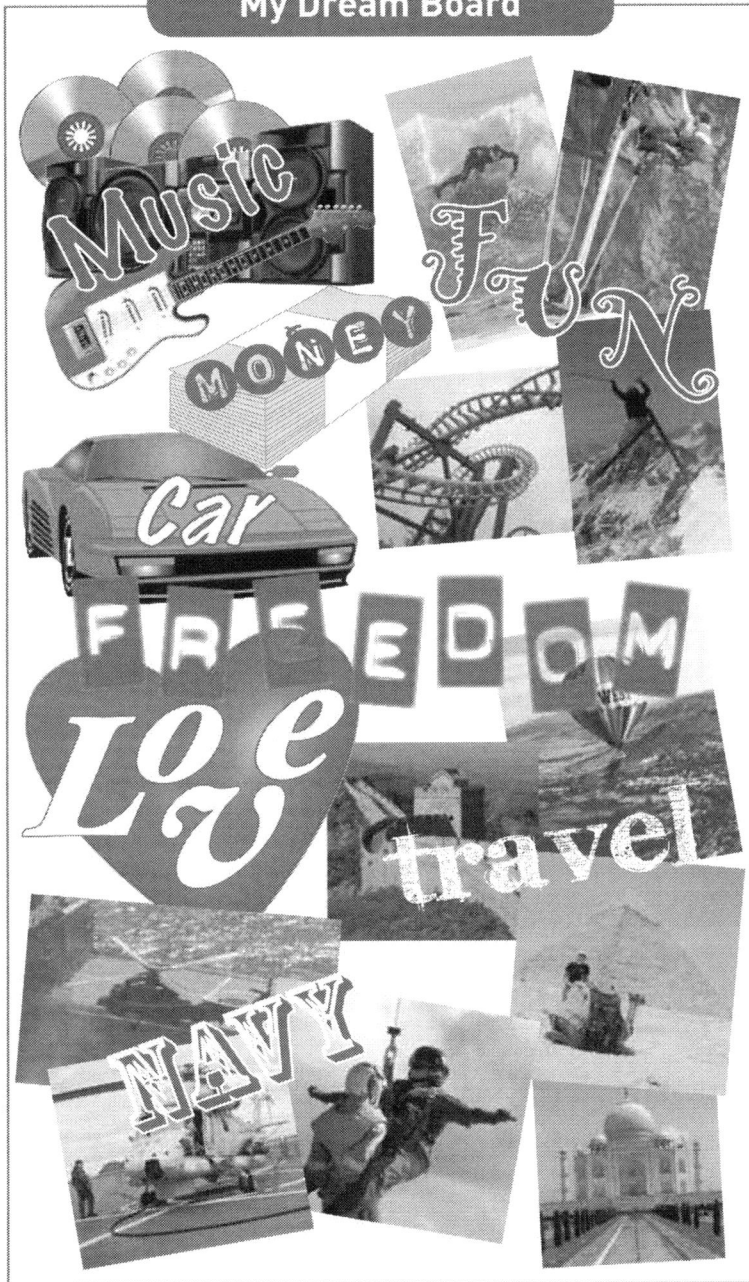

My Dream Board

Family activity idea 4.3

My 2011 (or 12, or 13) Dream (or Vision) Board

Here's what you and your children will need:

1 Two to three hours of uninterrupted time to relax and create, and some great music to create by.

2 A poster board. Half sheets work best, but if you want to use full sheets, by all means do so. Note: poster board generally has a shiny and a matt side. If you are going to be using Vivid markers, use the matt side as the shiny side smears (ask me how I know).

3 Lots of old/new magazines filled with great photos and large type (for ransom-note style cutout words). Magazines about your favourite hobbies and interests are great. Secondhand shops often have magazines for next to nothing if you don't have a stock on hand.

4 Tape, glue, scissors, markers and other art supplies for cutting out and attaching images to your poster board.

That's it. Just assemble the things you need, set aside the time for your whole family to create the next year of their lives (or more) the way everyone wants it – and have a great time.

Have each family member make a list of his/her goals. Here are some questions that may help your child to come up with a personal vision:

• What kind of house would you like to live in?

• What kind of car would you like to drive?

• What kind of clothes would you like to wear?

• What places would you like to visit?

• Would you like to have a private jet or spaceship?

• What kind of boat would you like to have?

• Who would you like to meet?

• Who are the people you would like to hang out with?

• What about your body – how healthy would you like to be?

• Are there any sports you would like to be good at?

• Are you interested in the arts – is there anything special you would like to achieve there?

• What kind of person would you like to be? Would you like to be more confident?

• Would you like to be kinder?

• How much money would you like to be earning every month?

52

- Which charities would you like to make a huge impact on?

- How many children would you like to have?

- How many and what kind of pets would you like to own?

- What does your future partner look like and what kind of character is he/she?

HINT: After everyone in the family has created their own dream or vision board and put it up on the wall, create a Family Dream Board for next year and put it on the fridge because refrigerators have magical powers. You don't know about that? Maybe I'll explain it later.

Now, go and plan your life! You'll be surprised at how much fun it is. And when things start coming true and showing up for you and your children, you will be even more excited about creating one for the following year.

Every morning, have a look at your dream boards and go over the family goals by having everyone say them out loud:

I am so happy and grateful now that ... I've built my dream house/I've filled my wardrobe with the most beautiful clothes/I'm the best player in my school's netball team/I've helped 50 people through my favourite charity by giving them the opportunity to eat healthy food...

The key is to have your children say this as if they've already accomplished their goals and dreams.

They need to convince their subconscious minds that their goals have already been achieved in order to make them become a reality. No one is ever successful until she absolutely believes in the depths of her soul that she's a success already! It is amazing how this simple dream board can make your child's dreams a reality – and yours too, of course.

The dream board serves as a constant reminder of why you're doing what you are to achieve your dreams. It will help you keep focused through the rough patches.

Parental role-modelling really makes a huge impact on your children. They will take their dream boards much more seriously if you have one too. And it's a lot of fun to see your dreams in front of you as if they've already come true!

54

Lesson 5

The traditional piggy bank is technically flawed

Introducing glass-jar budgeting

We've all done it. Looked at our young child or grandchild and thought, I'll buy him an adorable little piggy bank that he'll love and feed, and he'll grow up understanding that a penny saved is a penny earned.

It sounds good. It makes sense. It should work. But it doesn't. Why not? Piggy banks are technically flawed – they only have a slot dedicated to saving. They teach negative, dysfunctional, counter-productive attitudes to money, attitudes we don't fully comprehend until we're into our busy 20s, 30s, 40s and 50s and trying to raise a family.

Let's take a closer look at the negative and very limiting values that piggy banks teach:

- put all your money in one place

- leave it sitting there doing nothing

- when you want your money you have to break into the bank to get to it

- if you want to count your money, you have to do the same

- when you do finally access your money, you may find you have enough – or not. It's anyone's guess.

Would you run your household finances that way?

In addition to teaching negative attitudes to money, piggy banks are wildly impractical. They may be cute, but they are completely lacking in the banking basics that allow us to work with our money – and allow our money to work for us.

Instead of training our children to deal with money in a manner that's destined to fail for them as adults, we can choose to set up banks for them that teach them how to:

1. Separate money into compartments for different uses.

2. Invest, so that their money makes more money for them.

3. Share, so that their money can help others improve their lives.

4. Spend, at a level that fits within a budget and a plan.

5. Save for big-ticket items, so that large expenses are planned for, rather than coming as a surprise.

6. Take care of their physical money well, with a neat (and fun) place for coins and notes.

7. Count money regularly to mark progress toward goals, and to facilitate decision-making.

8. Understand the concept of Return On Investment (ROI), which many adults don't have a grasp of.

9. Be aware of compound interest, which many adults know of but don't fully understand.

10. Exercise their wealth habit muscles; if a child regularly works with a four-part wealth-building bank (instead of a piggy bank) when she's young, then she'll have a strong wealth-building muscle as an adult.

Piggy banks are cute but insidious programming devices with huge negative debt-ridden consequences. Your mission as a parent is to disable this device and replace it with a tool that builds wealth and character. Armed with the right information, you can raise financially savvy children by creating a see-through budgeting system they can learn.

For instance, how big is a trillion dollars? As $1 notes laid end-to-end, a trillion dollars would stretch approximately 109,219 kilometres, or 2.72 times around the equator.

If denominated in $100 notes, a trillion dollars would be enough to fill 4.5 Olympic-sized swimming pools, with a total volume of over 11,000 cubic metres.

Those visual images are not hard to understand and explain. Are the messages we send to our children about money this clear?

The invisible budgeting system

A typical family pays their bills online and pays for supermarket shopping and clothing with an eftpos or credit card. A person's pay is normally direct-credited. While all of this is very convenient, it creates an 'invisible budgeting system' that's not easy to teach. Children can't see the connections between working, earning and spending.

Children are naturally curious. They want to be involved and they want to understand the adult world. If you give them the opportunity to see how finances work, they will pick up personal finance and budgeting skills.

The glass-jar (or four-bank budgeting system)

Perhaps an old-fashioned budgeting system would serve our modern families well by providing the opportunity for children to see how things work. The 'glass-jar budgeting system' makes use of large preserving jars labelled for each expense: charitable giving, saving, housing, utilities, food, transportation, clothing, medical, personal and entertainment. After getting paid, you withdraw cash and the money for each is placed in its jar.

When there are special needs, extra jars are created. For example, a special jar is created for family holidays so planning for the extra expense is done in advance. This way the family can work together to save for the event, and everyone can see the progress made.

The glass jar system of budgeting allows children to understand the family finances. Money is right there for everyone to see and monitor. Where the money comes from is clear, and where it goes is also clear. There's no mystery.

As discussed in Lesson 1, it's good to teach children to compartmentalise money. Instead of using one bank, try four.

Family activity idea 5.1

Do you have to purchase four banks?

No. You can if you wish, but you can also start out this adventure with containers as simple as plastic Ziploc bags, so long as the kids can watch their money grow. You could use:

- Glass or clear-plastic jam or gherkin jars

- Plastic water or wide-mouth soft-drink bottles

- Cylindrical potato chip containers

Label each jar or bank

Take four containers and label them Save, Spend, Share and Grow.

Decorations: visual incentives

By turning the project into a fun activity, you make the message memorable. Decorate each bank using stickers, images cut from newspapers or magazines, or drawings to illustrate your child's money goals. What do you want to save for? Which cause do you want to support?

Back to basics

The four-bank idea will get you talking to your children in a very practical and comfortable way. You may find this system actually reminds you of the basics we as adults often forget when we're dealing with larger amounts. But be forewarned: as your children learn the principles of the four-bank system, they'll begin to watch more closely how you model money management at home. Your actions always speak louder than words!

Dividing money among banks

You should decide what part of your child's allowance or gift money should go into each of the four banks. Then stick to your plan, unless there are really good reasons to change. You are trying to teach your children a discipline that will protect them financially. If you are constantly adjusting or making exceptions, the child loses the sense of a system at work.

My glass jar formula: 10+30+30+30=Money savvy child

Take the four jars and line them up on a shelf. Each week when your child receives money, divide it up between the jars.

Take, for example, $10 pocket money.

First jar 10% Sharing – put in $1.

It's good to share and give to others. This is their Angel money, which is used every month to donate to charity, tithing at church or helping others in the community.

Second jar 30% Growing – put in $3.

This money is never spent, but invested in various ways to grow your child's wealth.

Third jar   30% Saving – put in $3.

This money is for your child to plan for and purchase more expensive items like a bike, game, X-box or computer.

Fourth jar   30% Spending – put in $3.

This is your child's wise spending budget for the month for toys, games, movies, ice cream, snacks or treats that he can buy on his own initiative.

The four-bank system teaches children to divide their money so they can use it in different ways. Use the following activity to help your children know where their money is heading.

Family activity idea 5.2

My budgeting diary

My budgeting diary for the week of _____

INCOME – money that comes in

Allowance: $ _____

Job: $ _____

Gifts: $ _____

Other: (description) $ _____

Other: (description) $ _____

Total income (A) $ _____

62

EXPENSES – money that goes out

Money for my Saving Jar $ _____

Money for my Spending Jar $ _____

Money for my Sharing Jar $ _____

Money for my Growing Jar $ _____

Clothes $ _____

Shoes $ _____

School lunches $ _____

Books $ _____

CDs $ _____

Snacks $ _____

Movie tickets $ _____

Other: (description) $ _____

Other: (description) $ _____

Other: (description) $ _____

Total expenses (B) $ _____

BUDGET SURPLUS/DEFICIT (A–B) $ _____

What I have left

Lesson 6

Allowances

To give or not to give

Do you consider giving your children pocket money or an allowance essential?

Is it bribery to ensure basic chores get done, or does it teach them budgeting, saving and basic money management skills? In truth, it's probably a bit of both, and I don't think either is a bad thing. Children watch and learn all the time, so start as soon as you can to model these money skills. Let children handle money and use the language of money when talking to them about shopping, or even a trip to the cash machine. In these days of credit cards, eftpos and internet banking, children rarely see money going out. But it comes in via ATMs, and of course eftpos cash-out – they could easily think you go shopping and get paid to do it!

Using pocket money and allowances as a starting point, you can develop important life skills. Children need to know that money comes into the household either as payment for work or as a benefit (often both), and that it's not a limitless supply. If their pocket money has limits, they can begin to learn to budget, save and think about how they want to spend the money.

They will also begin to learn that there are some jobs they are expected to do in the family for free, although there may well be others that offer financial reward. I have seen wide variations on the pocket money/allowance theme in terms of amounts, how it's earned and what it's spent on.

Children tend to get most of their money from their parents when and as it's needed, and occasionally by doing odd jobs. Here are some other ways children can obtain money, and the pluses and minuses attached to each.

Handouts

Money is given to a child when he/she asks for it. The drawback here is that the child doesn't learn to plan and save for future expenses. This practice may also promote begging, and makes it hard for parents to plan and track family spending.

Gifts

Children may receive money as gifts for birthdays or at holiday times, especially Christmas. Establish age-appropriate guidelines for children to follow before they receive money gifts. Guidelines might include how much gift money can be spent, how much should be saved and how much needs to be shared.

Remember, though, the money is the child's, and your child should make the final decision about how it will be used.

Rewards

Sometimes parents give money to children if they behave well or if they earn good marks at school. Such behaviour by the parents may give children the idea that all good behaviour and high achievements have a money price and should always be rewarded. Giving money for good behaviour or good marks is a bribe. From a developmental perspective, experts believe that giving monetary rewards is not something that a parent should do.

If you do decide to give money as a reward, make it unplanned and unannounced – a pleasant surprise. Money shouldn't be used as a reward past the age of 11 or 12. By then, rewards should be internal. If a child does a good job cleaning the bathroom, compliment the child's effort and mention how good he/she must feel. An occasional, spontaneous family night out to celebrate good marks can be a morale booster. Even adults are rewarded when winning scholarships, getting a pay rise at work for doing a good job, or being promoted. Help children learn that rewards for achievements happen occasionally, and can't be counted on every time.

Paid work

From the lemonade stand to the suburban car wash, chores and jobs are a great way for children to learn how money is made. Earnings are the money children receive for doing jobs beyond what is expected as a family member. If children are to be paid for special work done at home, set the price and the standards for the job before it's started. For example, if a child is going to clean out a shed and she will be paid, tell her before she starts how much she will receive and your expectations. Consider paying a child for jobs outsiders might be paid to do, such as raking leaves, mowing grass, baby-sitting or weeding.

Earning gives children a sense of freedom and recognition and leads to financial independence. You can help your children establish excellence in work standards before they work away from home, and help them find work suitable for their age and skills. (Stop a child's earnings if it interferes with school or other things important to the child and family.) You will learn more about how your children can earn the old-fashioned way in the next lesson.

Chore-based earnings

Some parents believe children should be required to earn their pocket money by doing chores so they will begin to appreciate the value of money. When work performed equates to money, children learn quickly to prioritise their desires. It is much easier to request a new toy when Mum and Dad are picking up the tab; when a child must earn part (or all) of the money and save for special items, they begin to view money in a whole new way.

Family activity idea 6.1

Chore Charts – the ultimate reward mechanism

Chore charts are probably the easiest way to organise and track chore-based earnings. You can use a simple calendar to keep track of completed chores and their values. Here are some chore-chart tips to help you get started:

• Payments are usually made each week upon the completion of agreed tasks.

• Make a list of all the chores that need to get done around the house: weeding the garden, washing the car, sweeping the garage, dusting the living room. (I personally feel that making your bed and doing the dishes are non-paying, must-do on a daily basis chores.)

• Put a dollar amount next to each chore.

• Your children can then pick and choose which chores (based on how much money they need this week or month) they want to do. Chores must pass inspection before payment.

68

• This gives your children the freedom to choose their extra-credit chores, the freedom to make some extra cash when needed, and encourages them to take pride in their work.

Chore Chart

Name: ....

For (date / week): ....

Chore	Brush teeth	Clean up toys	Put away shoes	Make bed	Sort laundry
Sunday					
Monday					
Tuesday					
Wednesday					
Thursday					
Friday					
Saturday					
Total					

You can name the icons as you wish; I've tried to be generic, but of course, everything is open to interpretation with children.

Brush
teeth

Clean up
toys

Finish
homework

Fold
laundry

Hang
laundry

Make
bed

Put away
books

Set
table

Put away
shoes

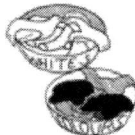

Sort
dirty laundry

Sweep/mop
floor

Wash
dishes

Water
plants

Get mail/
newspaper

Put on/take off
jacket

Feed
pet(s)

Wash
hands

Go
potty

Age-appropriate chores for children

Ages two and three

Many toddlers are eager to help with chores, and while their 'helping' may not always be appreciated, you should cherish their excitement and keep alive their habit of helping. Sticker charts are a great way to keep toddlers excited about helping. Their chores may have to be completed with you helping every step of the way, but you are laying the groundwork for children who regard chores and helping as a way of life.

Some chores two- to three-year-olds can do:

- help make the bed
- pick up toys and books
- take laundry to the laundry room
- help feed pets
- help wipe up messes
- dust with socks on their hands
- mop in areas with help.

Ages four and five

Preschoolers still enjoy helping and are usually thrilled when time is taken to teach them new chores. They are ready to do some chores without constant supervision. Rewards at this age are very motivating. A sticker chart that allows them to build up to bigger rewards can be appropriate. For some preschoolers, tying chores to an allowance is a great option and fosters independence in choosing a reward.

Some additional chores preschoolers can do:

- clearing and setting the table
- dusting
- helping with cooking and preparing food
- carrying and putting away groceries.

Ages six to eight

These school-age children may or may not still have their childlike enthusiasm for completing chores. What they do have, however, is an overwhelming desire to be independent. Parents and caregivers can guide children to become independent in their chores, using chore charts to keep track of their responsibilities, both completed and pending.

Some additional chores for school-age children:

- taking care of pets
- vacuuming and mopping
- taking out the rubbish
- folding and putting away laundry.

Ages nine to 12

Children at this pre-teen stage are capable of increasing responsibility where chores are concerned.

Keep in mind that they tend to need continuity. Find a system that works for your family and don't change it without the input and support of the people it affects. Make sure you factor in rewards and consequences, and address those issues with your children. Let them know the consequences of not completing chores, as well as the rewards for fulfilling their responsibilities.

Some additional chores for pre-teens:

- helping wash the car

- learning to wash dishes

- helping prepare simple meals

- cleaning the bathroom

- raking leaves

- operating the washer and dryer.

Ages 13 to 17
Teenagers are developmentally ready to handle almost any chore in the home. At the same time, a teenager's schedule can sometimes become quite hectic, leaving little time for chores. Make sure that the workload of your teenagers is manageable.

Some additional chores for teenagers:

- replace light bulbs and vacuum cleaner bags

- all aspects of the laundry

- wash windows

- clean out the fridge and wipe other kitchen appliances

- prepare meals

- prepare grocery shopping lists.

Remember that children mature at their own pace and not all children will be capable of advanced chores at the same age, just as some children may be ready for more difficult chores at a younger age. The most important guidelines are supervision and evaluation of your child's needs and abilities.

Allowances

Allowances help children learn how to handle money. Budgeting and allowances help them to avoid being victims of money and to be in control of their financial futures.

Some parents teach their children through a weekly allowance. Make sure to give your child a raise for added responsibilities. Parents often give a set amount of money to children on a regular basis (for example, $5 a week). This allows children to learn how to save, spend and share. It also lets them set their own financial goals.

How to calculate your child's allowance

This is almost certainly the first hurdle. Some parents give their children a dollar for every year of their age, i.e. a five-year-old gets $5. But do what you feel comfortable with and can afford.

As a starting point you may want to look at an amount that will buy a small treat, e.g. packet of lollies, pencils, stickers etc.

Younger children
A good (and fair) way to calculate your child's allowance, especially when you have more than one, is to take the child's age and halve it. For example, if your child is six, her allowance is $3 a month (if you can afford it, you may want to make it $3 a week). This is fun for your children because they know each birthday brings them a raise in their allowance.

Older siblings
The older they are the more money they get, as per the age-based allowance described above. For older children, it may be wise to agree to make adjustments for special cases, such as an upcoming school trip where more spending money might be helpful.

Sit down with older children and ask them to suggest an amount based on research they have done on the price of those things which are to be included in the pocket money/allowance remit. This is a good exercise for them as they begin to see how their money will stretch.

Remember it is important that they learn how to save, so the money has to be spread out over the course of the year!

Allowance ground rules

If you decide to give your child an allowance, here are some things to keep in mind:

- Stick to a regular schedule. Give your child the same amount of money on the same day each week.

- Sit down and set goals together with your children.

- Picture their dreams!

- Children have different values. Let them take the lead in identifying their goals. Don't forget to set goals for saving, spending and sharing.

- Create a budget. Working with a budget early on in life helps children experience success with money and a sense of empowerment.

- Begin by designating a percentage of their allowance as free spending money. This gives them a taste of personal freedom. Lesson 5 looks in more detail at how to divide up your child's allowance.

- You can start small children saving with the system outlined in Lesson 5; older children can open a savings account, or if you are share market and managed fund savvy, get them investing early and on a regular basis.

- Have the children give a percentage to charity. McDonald's takes donations for the Ronald McDonald House, and most local supermarkets display cans for numerous other charities.

- Help your children keep track of transactions and allocations – remind your child to keep his/her goals in mind by using the Goal Tracker discussed in Lesson 4.

- It's important for children to make mistakes and learn from them in order to set reasonable goals.

- Consider giving a raise to reward your child for handling his or her allowance well.

- You should renegotiate allowances each year.

Healthy financial habits begin with the small successes and failures that come out of managing an allowance. Giving children the opportunity to experience the ups and downs of budgeting helps ensure a more stable future and financial independence.

Some extra tips:

- Encourage your child/children to earn extra money as early as possible.

- Negotiate the price for different tasks, and make the amount earned relate to the difficulty of the task.

- Explain that as they get older they will be expected to do some of these tasks for free, but you will provide opportunities for them to earn money doing other tasks.

- Once they are teenagers they can begin to earn money doing various jobs outside the home. Support them in this process.

- Once they are earning their own money allow them to spend it on whatever they want. Remind them of things they may need to save up for, or want to purchase as extras. In some instances you may want to negotiate part-payment, e.g. you provide half the holiday spending money and they save the rest.

- Be realistic. If you know how much things cost and can explain how you budget the household accounts, they will understand the need for doing the same with their own money. They will also understand why you can only afford a certain amount for them.

- Don't be offended if they suggest ways you could cut down on your own spending. This might well be part of their arguments for more money. Children learn through parental modelling, and if you are modelling good money management (and you can do this even if you are in debt), they will see the decisions you make in a positive light, and understand your financial situation.

- If you are short of money for a period of time, explain this and the reasons for the deficit (obviously this depends on the age of the child). Negotiate a cut in their allowance if necessary, although this should only be in proportion to the amount you are cutting back as well. But be prepared, if necessary, to stop their money for a period if this is going to help a crisis or debt situation. Again, do this in discussion with them and find ways of enabling them to earn the difference, supporting them in whatever ways you can.

Family activity idea 6.2

Create an allowance contract

Creating an allowance contract is the next step in the process. Before you give your child the allowance, sit down together and work out a simple contract. In the contract, you promise to give a set amount of allowance on a given day of the week. In return, your child promises to:

• save a predetermined percentage of the allowance

• put the savings in the bank at the end of the month

• not withdraw savings from the bank for the first three months

• spend the savings on items related to the goals he has set.

Committing to these promises teaches your child about developing good financial habits, setting goals and making a commitment. Making the allowance contract is a lot of fun, and gives your child the opportunity to ask lots of questions about money. You'll be surprised at the questions children ask.

Allowance contract

Child I, ... will:

1 Receive $ .... allowance every ....

2 Put .... % into my Saving Jar   .... % into my Spending Jar

   .... % into my Sharing Jar   .... % into my Growing Jar

   when I receive my allowance

3 Visit the bank with Mum / Dad on the last .... of the month to deposit my savings

4 Withdraw savings only after a minimum of $ .... is reached

5 Create a wish list setting out what the allowance and savings will be used for.

Parent I, ... will:

1 Pay $ .... allowance every ....

2 Receive a copy of the wish list detailing what the allowance will be used for

3 Receive a plan of what savings will be used for, both short and long term.

I, ... will use my allowance for:

....

....

....

I, ... will use my savings for:

....

....

....

Signed,

Child ....   Parent ....

Date ...... / ...... / ......   Date ...... / ...... / ......

73

Family activity idea 6.3
The allowance tracker

To help you be consistent in your allowance programme, I suggest you keep a written record of what you've given out. This is a visual reminder of what has been spent on your children. I recommend that you keep track for a two-week period. Listed opposite are some categories to help you. After two weeks, take the average.

Let's say your usual night to give out allowances is Monday, and you realise at nine o'clock in the evening that not only have you forgotten to pay, but you don't have enough cash in your wallet. It's late, it's raining and you decide to pay the allowance on Tuesday instead. Then, before you know it, it's Friday and you can't remember if you paid the allowance this week or not. Keeping a record enables you to figure out when you last paid, and how much. In addition, when your child comes to you to nag about not having received their allowance 'for at least three weeks' you can produce the proof and the discussion is over. You'll either apologise and pay out, or smile smugly.

This tracking method is especially helpful if there are several children in the family, or if you have a shared parenting arrangement.

Don't be tempted

It may be hard, but don't relent when your child asks for more money. She has to learn that money does not flow from the ATM in endless amounts. Be consistent. Stick to the allowance contract.

Amount of money spent each day

Child's name	Categories	1	2	3	4	5	6	7	8	9	10	11	12	13	14	Total	Average

Lesson 7

Work isn't a dirty word

Earning money the old-fashioned way

'But I want it NOW!'

It's as if yelling this over and over gives a child – or an adult – the right to whatever they want, when they want it. Veruca Salt in *Charlie and the Chocolate Factory* demonstrates the undesirability of children getting what they want, when they want it. The spoilt girl demands her father get her a squirrel that can sort good walnuts from bad, just like the ones she sees in the chocolate factory. When she learns the squirrels aren't for sale, little Veruca helps herself. As a result she (and her father) are tossed out with the rest of the bad nuts.

Why does Veruca think she deserves whatever she wants? It's simple. Her father has always given in to her every wish.

Learning the value of money

There's a story about a boy who came from a wealthy family. His father had built a multimillion-dollar business from the ground up. As the father approached retirement, he told his son that he wanted him to take over the company. Pleased, the son asked, 'When are you going to give it to me?' The father said, 'I'm not going to give you anything, you must earn it.' The son asked, 'How am I supposed to do that?'

The father answered, 'First, you must earn $10,000 to purchase a small portion of ownership in the company. After this is accomplished, you will get your next instruction.' As the son was about to begin his quest, his mother thrust $10,000 into his hand and told him to give the money to his father. Thrilled by his good fortune, he looked for his father. The old man was sitting by the fire reading a book. The son said, 'Dad, here's $10,000.' The father took the money, tossed it on the fire and watched it burn. The son was frozen in amazement, but his father said, 'Come back when you have earned the money!'

As he set out, his mother again thrust $10,000 into his hand. This time she told him he needed to convince his father he'd worked for the money. So the boy scuffed himself up a little, jogged around the block a few times, and then went to find his father again. His father was still sitting by the fire reading a book. The boy approached him and said, 'It sure is tough earning money. Here's the $10,000. I really do want to own the business.' Once again his father took the money and tossed it into the fireplace. As it burned, the son asked, 'How did you know I didn't earn that money?' His father said, 'It's easy to lose or spend money that isn't your own.'

At this point, the son realised he wasn't going to get the business unless he actually earned the $10,000. So when his mother offered him money again, he declined. He went out and picked up some odd jobs. His jobs required him to get up early and stay up late, but he worked and worked until he'd finally earned $10,000. Proudly, he presented his father with the money. But as before, his father threw it on the fire. As the flames began to devour the banknotes the son, risking severe burns, stuck his hands into the fire and pulled out as much money as he could rescue. The father looked his son in the eyes and said, 'I see you really did earn the money this time.'

The earning mentality versus the entitlement mentality

Many parents make the mistake of providing financial assistance to their children. Their motives are usually good. They want to help their children get started in life or assist them when a financial crisis arises. Unfortunately, the result is often the opposite to the one desired. Instead of helping children become self-sufficient, they become dependent. Rather than learning initiative and discipline, the children become idle and self-indulgent. Instead of being achievement-oriented, they become entitlement-oriented, ungrateful and demanding. Children who always get what they want will want as long as they live. Thomas J. Stanley and William D.

Danko in *The Millionaire Next Door* claim research has shown that 'in general, the more dollars adult children receive [from their parents], the fewer they accumulate, while those who are given fewer dollars accumulate more.'

The common thread in Stanley and Danko's book is that people destined to become wealthy are very careful about using credit and tend to save for things before they buy them. The average millionaire in this book drives a second-hand family car and lives in a middleclass suburb, and not necessarily in the best house in the street. The majority of these wealthy people weren't members of exclusive private golf or yacht clubs, and most sent their children to state schools. The average millionaire interviewed would describe himself as a 'tightwad', spending no more money than was absolutely necessary.

How can we make sure our children grow up with the earning mentality rather than the entitlement mentality?

A few years ago, a friend of mine started his first business and he often relied on one of his business partners and mentors, who was a multimillionaire, for advice. His business was growing but struggled to turn a profit. He continued to work hard but things were getting tougher and tougher financially. He went to his rich partner and asked for a loan to help him get by until the business was profitable. The request was declined. Frustrated, my friend said, 'You're making millions a year and I'm struggling to stay afloat. Please help me.' He could tell the other man wanted to help; in fact he was close to giving in to my friend's plea, but he said, 'If I take away your struggle, I'll also take away your victory.' And he shared the following story.

'A young boy came across a caterpillar in a cocoon. He visited the cocoon several times each day, waiting for the butterfly to emerge, and after a few days he saw the cocoon move as the butterfly struggled to emerge. Wanting to help, the boy ran home for a pair of scissors. He carefully cut open the cocoon and out fell a partially developed butterfly, which would never fly. With the best of intentions, the boy had killed the butterfly he was trying to help.'

At the time, my friend didn't find this advice helpful, but today he is grateful to a wise mentor who resisted the temptation to cut open his cocoon.

The value of work

One of the best ways to create an earning mentality in our children is to teach them how to work. However, as more parents are providing financially for their children's needs, fewer young people are learning to work. In 2007, for the first time on record, the majority of Australian and New Zealand teenagers were not working or looking for work at the beginning of the summer. On average, only 48% of teens aged 16 to 19 were working or looking for work in June

2007, a steep decline from the 66% of teens doing so in June 1978, according to census data.

Work helps overcome a false sense of entitlement. I have identified three significant factors that impart good work ethics. Parents need to look for opportunities to assign or create chores and work for children that have the following characteristics:

Purpose

The job assigned must have a real purpose. When I was a child, there was a large vacant plot of land behind our house that was covered in weeds. My dad divided up the plot and gave each of us children a section. Our instructions were simply to pull the weeds by hand. I can remember hating this job. It was always hot and dusty, and the weeds grew fast and tall.

When I asked why we had to keep the weeds down, Dad explained that it was to prevent them spreading into the yard and garden so the grass would be soft to play on and the garden would grow lots of good food to eat. This gave me a purpose I was willing to work for. I still didn't like weeding but, understanding the purpose of the job, I had motivation.

Sometimes parents give children meaningless 'busywork'. This may be better than watching TV or playing video games all day, but jobs with real purpose will ignite a feeling of true accomplishment and a sense of contribution to a greater good.

Consistency

Parents need to be consistent in assigning chores. If making the bed is an important skill or chore you want your child to learn then you must be consistent in giving the assignment every day, and just as consistent in following up to make sure the job is done well. If you do so, the child will be likely to match your consistency.

Good work ethics are taught by this kind of consistency. Punctuality is important in the workplace and in life. It wasn't until I got my first job outside the home, at a department store while I was a student, that I learnt to appreciate the need to be at work on time. Those who've had jobs while still in college tend to have a stronger work ethic than those who haven't. This leads me to believe that teaching children to work is also teaching them a way of life.

Perseverance

One of the hardest things in life is to continue doing something when it's no longer fun – or when it was never fun to begin with. The world is inclined to teach our children that such discomfort shouldn't be tolerated. It is, on the contrary, how good work ethics are learned. It is important to teach our youth to continually work past the point of comfort. Not many reach this point regularly, but it is here that character is permanently built. Learning good work ethics involves persevering through the discomfort and beyond the pain of work.

I have a friend who worked at a timber mill. His job was to stack timber as it came off the saw. This was the most physically demanding job he'd ever had. At the end of each day he was utterly drained, baked by the summer heat in the sawmill and exhausted by the effort of keeping up with the saw as it relentlessly kicked out timber to be stacked. It was just a miserable job, but he came to see that it was a job that had to be done and gradually he acquired a sense of pride in doing it well.

If you protect your children from struggle and responsibility, you will also prevent them from growing. Help your child learn how to work and earn by assigning work that has real purpose, consistency and requires perseverance. A work ethic and the earning mentality cannot be purchased with money, but are developed through experience, responsibility and education. The entitlement mentality is a form of bondage, for it is simply living off others. Give your children education and opportunity rather than money, and teach them how to work.

One day, your child will need to earn a living. Children can get an edge on the work world by starting early and in doing so they will gain valuable experience by working with different people, learning about managing money, perhaps putting some aside for their tertiary education. A paper round, mowing lawns, baby-sitting or doing odd jobs will not only earn your children money but also teach them important life skills. But first ask yourself if your child is ready to work. Does he have the time, or will it interfere with his school work?

Many children would like to start earning some money. Encouraging your children to work is a great way to foster creativity and innovation, to promote independence and teach them key financial skills like budgeting, saving, managing money and investing.

Finding a job

There are a variety of part-time jobs for teenagers. But if your children aren't old enough to be hired by an employer, here are some alternative ways to make money.

Starting at home

Consider tasks that need to be done around your home or at your work that go beyond basic household chores. Does the car need washing? Are there leaves to rake or lawns to mow? Or can you delegate to your child a task that you would ordinarily do yourself, like gift wrapping, typing an email (which you can dictate), or making greeting cards?

If you have a family-run business, consider ways to get your children involved that are age-appropriate and would give them a sense of accomplishment and involvement.

Look to your community

Most jobs are found through word of mouth, so encourage your child to let relatives, family friends and neighbours know that she is in the market for work. Offering to do odd jobs for people you know and trust – gardening work, lawnmowing, dog walking, pet and/or baby-sitting – is a great place to start. Or encourage your child to sell unwanted toys or books at a garage sale or outdoor market. They will learn valuable financial skills as well as making a few dollars.

List skills and abilities

If your child wants a job, help her compile a list of skills, abilities, likes and dislikes. This brainstorming exercise is great for children and adults alike, and encourages your child to think creatively.

If your child enjoys art, why not make and sell greeting cards? If he enjoys cooking, why not hold a baking sale or even start a business selling cookies? If your child is more academically inclined, suggest tutoring younger children. Tutoring is a great way to reinforce existing knowledge and will help develop interpersonal and mentoring skills.

Encourage the young entrepreneur

Children are increasingly showing interest in learning about investing and starting their own businesses. There are a growing range of educational tools, websites and investment programmes available, with organisations even offering camps for young entrepreneurs. Be sure to do your research before deciding on a particular website or camp – ensure that you choose one that is appropriate for your child.

Helping your children discover creative ways to make money is also teaching them key financial lessons about budgeting, saving and investing for the future.

Some suggested jobs for children

Some at least of the following opportunities may be available in your community:

Baby-sitter Parents often need a reliable baby-sitter. This role can even be expanded by getting together a group of older children who can offer baby-sitting services to all the parents in your street. Make sure, however, that you know who they're working for.

Parent helper If your child isn't old enough to do baby-sitting, a job helping parents with feeding or entertaining younger children, or doing chores around the house, offers another possibility. Your child will also likely gain some references for regular baby-sitting work later on.

House cleaner   Instead of helping with younger children, your child may be able to do housework like vacuuming or dusting.

Lemonade stand operator   This is a seasonal business of course, and the possibilities depend on your location. During winter, it could be a warm-drink business – but be careful if your child needs to handle hot items. Children may want to branch out into selling coffee, muffins, scones, donuts or snack bags. Setting up a booth at a local community fair, if that is allowed, is a good way to get started.

Apart from food, consider other items that could be sold. Is your child good at crafts? Could she create her own jewellery to sell, or decorate interesting rocks? Sometimes, a combination of food and artwork can make a good business.

Car-wash operator   Suggest that your child get together with friends to offer to wash local cars. As an add-on to this business, they may be able to sell the kind of items discussed in the lemonade stand section above to people waiting while their car is washed. See what professional car-wash services charge in your area, and price competitively.

Animal care If your child enjoys animals, what about an animal care business? This might involve walking dogs, washing them or general grooming.

House and/or pet-sitter   If a neighbour is taking a trip or holiday, taking care of their house and/or pets may provide an opportunity. This might include watering plants, collecting mail and so on.

Landscape gardener Cutting grass, weeding, trimming, planting flowers and other landscaping jobs are often available. Scan the neighbourhood for homes that need landscaping services. In the spring, offer to plant flowers or do a post-winter clean-up.

Tips for running the business

For many of these small-business activities, your children could print and hand out flyers to be distributed in the neighbourhood. As the business grows, testimonials can be quoted. Giving free samples is always a good way to attract business. For services, offer coupons for potential new customers.

Safety first

The most important consideration for parents of children offering goods and services in the community is to ensure their safety. Don't allow them to be involved in any of these activities unless they are old enough to work with you in following these important guidelines:

- You must always know where they are.

- They should never go door-to-door by themselves.

- Recommend that they seek jobs they will feel confident doing. Be sure they are mentally prepared and committed to the work they are being paid to do.

- If there is a cost in setting up the business, make sure they have enough money and know where the money is coming from.

- Paid work should never interfere with normal school work or completing homework.

- Help them set fair prices for the work they are doing. Tell them to come to you for advice if they need it.

Family activity idea 7.1

All in a day's work

Look at the following list of occupations with your child. Ask him to rank them according to income, i.e. write 1 next to the person who they think earns the most, through to 12 for the lowest paid occupation. For younger children you may have to explain some occupations. Then ask the child to guess what someone in each of these occupations might earn for a day's work.

Professional rugby player	$ _____
Butcher	$ _____
Baker/cook	$ _____
Actor/actress on TV (not a superstar)	$ _____
The Prime Minister	$ _____
Veterinarian	$ _____
Police officer	$ _____
Dentist	$ _____
TV news anchor	$ _____
Hairdresser/stylist	$ _____
Paediatrician	$ _____

Family activity idea 7.2

More or less

1 Sit down with your child and focus on a recent or anticipated family purchase. The item should represent a moderate to large part of the family budget. This could be a new television, another appliance, furniture, a car or a family holiday.

2 Write the most likely (or the actual) purchase item in the centre of a lined piece of paper. For example, list a new, moderately priced sedan on the line in the centre of the page.

3 Write the word LESS on the line beneath the purchase item. Ask your children and other family members to brainstorm alternatives that would cost less. For example, a used car, repairing the car you already have, public transport, riding a bike or walking.

4 Write the word MORE on the line above the purchase item. Now brainstorm possible substitutes that would cost more. For example, a luxury sedan, a basic SUV or a luxury SUV.

5 Take the show on the road by visiting a car dealership (or an appliance or furniture store), or visit car dealers, furniture stores or appliance stores on-line. Find similar items that cost more, or less.

6 Point out that when families make spending decisions, they MUST consider their income. The amount of income we earn gives us choices; however, it also sets limits. Families must consider the options available within the limits.

Lesson 8

Your child doesn't like to save?

Try the carrot and then the stick

Did you ever dream about owning a Porsche?

Did you ever want to put a pool in your back yard (or want to acquire a back yard to put one in)? An adult's financial goals generally require a heavy savings commitment. Grown-ups save to buy a home, start a family, maybe start a business and enjoy a comfortable retirement. Those who are successful in meeting their goals generally are the ones who are experienced in saving. These people learnt about saving early on.

You can help your children get the things they want by teaching them about saving. Unless they were born with a miser gene, they would probably prefer to spend, spend, spend. But there's as much – or more – satisfaction from saving as from spending, as long as children know what the payoff will be. They need to understand that they will never have financial maturity if they don't have good saving habits.

Teaching your children to save is an important part of parenting. Children can learn the principles at a young age. When they get money for birthdays, holidays, odd jobs and/or allowances, help them to resist the urge to spend by showing them the long-term benefits of saving. Help them pick an item, one that might take a few months to save for. Encourage a sense of anticipation, make saving exciting, and children will be more willing to hold onto their money.

Here are a few tips to get you started:

- save a percentage of the money made in a week, as explained in Lesson 5

- save spare change

- match your child's savings.

Teaching children to save early and often should help establish a habit they'll carry into adult life. They could perhaps save 10% (or more) of their allowance, or all the change they have (and only spend notes). If you have the money to match their savings (or even if you put in 10c to their $1), this will give them a bigger incentive to squirrel away their dollars.

Where to save

Younger children may not understand the banking concept, seeing banks as institutions that take money but don't give it back. You can help your child save money by starting at home. Use the glass jar system (see Lesson 5), or even a plastic bag where they can see their money grow. Once the child has a small store of money, you might want to open a savings account in his or her name. Find the right bank and the right savings account and take your child to the bank. Illustrate how you make deposits and show them that you can also withdraw the money (though not the exact same notes and coins).

Banks generally require a parent or guardian to co-sign. Also, your child may not be able to withdraw money without your signature, so you may have to be their personal banker until they turn 18.

Parental input

Goals can be powerful motivators, but children often need a little nudging to stay on track. They are likely to veer off-track here and there, tempted by a fashion fad perhaps. That's okay, but you can help keep them up to the mark by:

1. Reminding them that spending on a whim will make their goals more distant. What does that mean in dollars and time? But don't push; this is a learning experience. Up to a point, the more you try to control them, the less they learn.

2. Sweetening the pot with some saving incentives. If your child's goal is particularly constructive and worthy, you can offer to kick in a certain amount.

You can double the bank's interest rate, you can offer them a challenge grant (once they save half, you'll contribute the other half, or whatever you're willing to shell out), or set up a matching grant, either dollar-for-dollar or whatever you feel inspired and able to contribute.

You should set a few rules to make this technique more effective. If your child decides to withdraw some money, you stop matching contributions until he replaces it; that way, you're not always putting in and he's not always taking out – at least not without consequences. And keep careful track (or if your child is old enough, have your child keep track) of inflows and outflows. The table below shows how this can work.

Date	Child's deposit	Parent's match	Withdrawals	Repayment balance	Total
1/1	$10	$10	—	—	$20
29/1	$5	$5	—	—	$30
12/2	—	—	$12	$12	$18
26/2	$4	—	—	$8	$22
12/3	$10	$2	—	—	$34

Forcing children to save

Many parents force children to save 10%, 30% or even half of their allowance, earnings and gift money. And it works – at least until they hit their rebellious teens, when they're bound to insist, 'It's my money, I can do what I want with it!' And they're right.

The other issue is that some children, when they leave home, will sigh with relief. At last they won't have to save any more!

The goal is to get them to *want* to save. Forcing them may succeed while they're under your roof, but it won't necessarily make savers of them once they're out on their own. And that's when saving becomes most important.

Inspiring children to save

You can guide your children to develop lifelong saving habits by helping them to set goals that are meaningful to them. Use your children's interests. If your daughter loves skiing or playing the guitar, for instance, and she falls in love with a $400 pair of skis or a new guitar, make it a saving goal.

Say she gets $15 a week allowance, $5 of which you've earmarked as discretionary. Help her identify different strategies:

- **Save all of it** (forgoing music, movies and pizza with friends) It'll take about 20 months to save up for the item. That's beyond most children's (and adults') tolerance for delayed gratification. Consider this a benchmark against which to rate other strategies.

- **Get a job** If your daughter began baby-sitting or got herself a paper run, earning $20 a week, she could save $400 in 20 weeks.

- **Save and work** Add $5 of weekly discretionary allowance to the $20 earnings, and she can save $400 in 16 weeks.

For younger children set more modest goals – things they can save for in much shorter time periods. Offer to let them do extra chores (on top of the usual household chores for which they're not paid) to help them earn and save faster. Tape a picture of what they're saving for onto their bank, and chart their progress visually, perhaps with a picture of a thermometer or an hourglass that they can colour in as they progress.

Withdrawals

Children need to understand why they are saving. Usually that means getting a tangible reward at the end for holding onto their money. You need to decide if you want your children's savings accounts to be for future needs, or simply to teach them the concept of saving.

If a child puts only a percentage of her money into savings, then she can use the remainder in a discretionary way. Another arrangement involves setting a minimum balance on the child's savings account. She can withdraw money as long as her balance stays above, for example, $100.

There's nothing wrong with wishing

Does your child always seem to be asking for something? There's nothing inherently wrong in wanting material things, and having a definite goal serves as an incentive for achieving it.

So let your child dream, as long as he understands it's up to him to make his dreams come true. The Dream Board concept we talked about in Lesson 4 comes in handy here.

Watch your step

Don't undermine your child's savings resolve by buying the thing she's saving for. You may satisfy your child's desires today, but you're teaching her that she doesn't have to save to get what she wants.

Piggybank on it

When estimating the cost of the things your children want, it's better to err on the high side. The worst that will happen is that your children reach their goals sooner. If the target savings figure is too low, your children won't save enough to reach their goal.

Making a wish list

A wish list is just a way of putting down financial goals on paper. According to one survey, teenage boys typically save up for a car, teenage girls for university, while younger children have no particular savings goals. Your child can learn to become a more determined saver by deciding what he's saving for.

Use the sheets in section entitled "Making wishes come true" to list your child's goals. You'll see that there are two sheets: short-term and long-term. Short-term goals are ones that can be reached in a matter of weeks or a couple of months. Long-term goals can take several months or even years to attain. A young child will probably only have short-term goals. That's okay. Having short-term goals is enough to get them started on the road to saving success. The important thing is that children have some sort of goal so they can develop the savings habit.

Making wishes come true

Once your children know what they want, you'll need to help them put a price tag on it. For example, if they want to save up for the school ball, make sure they add in all the expenses involved (tickets, suit hire, corsage, limo, after-ball party and so on).

Having a savings goal is only half the battle; your child must know how much she needs to save to reach her goal. There are different ways to figure this out.

- **Use a regular savings plan** Decide how much of each allowance or pay will be set aside, regardless of the savings goals. Then the item can be purchased when the goal is met. For example, if your daughter starts baby-sitting, you may want to put half of everything aside for long-term goals. She can either save or spend the rest. This 50/50 rule works well, giving her a worthwhile bank account when she gets to university.

- **Save as much as possible** Supplement a regular savings plan with additional savings. This way, your child will reach his goal when he's saved what's needed. For example, if something costs $100 and your child's regular savings amount is $5 a week, then it will take 20 weeks (or about five months) to reach the goal. But if he gets an extra $5 here or $10 there, saving time can be cut considerably.

Short-term goal worksheet

I'm saving for the next .... months for the following goal(s):

Draw or stick pictures
of your goal(s) here

A description of my goal(s):

My goal(s) will cost: $ ....

Family activity idea 8.2

Long-term goal worksheet

I'm saving / investing for the next .... months / years for the following goal(s):

A description of my goal(s):

My goal(s) will cost: $ ....

- **Back into a target savings amount**   If your child knows how long it takes to save for something, she can divide the dollars needed by the time it will take. For example, if it's going to cost $500 to go to the ball and it's the August before your daughter's senior year, she'll have 10 months in which to save for this big expense. That means she'll need to put $50 aside each month to pay for ball expenses.

Targeting a savings amount is most effective for the big ticket items she's saving for. You'll see that in a minute when it comes to saving for university.

Family activity idea 8.3

Create a saving bank/glass jar for money to grow so that it can be used later

Watch it grow together When you save money, it grows. That's the first message you can help your child understand. You can easily drop coins into the bank, illustrating how at the end of four weeks the amount within the bank has grown. (This is the advantage of a bank with transparent walls. Children can watch their money accumulate.)

Coins grow into notes When you save, coins turn into notes. Empty the bank and cash-in four weeks' worth of coins for paper money. Put the notes back in the bank, along with the extra change.

Keep saving – and the money grows When you save over time, money really grows. Now show how the amount of money builds over several months. Drop in coins, count them weekly and trade them for notes.

You earn something called interest Savings plus interest equals even more money. Talk to your child about interest – begin by explaining that interest is the money a bank pays savers for holding their money. You can illustrate the idea by adding 10 cents to each dollar your child saves. Count out $10 in single dollar coins, then place ten 10-cent pieces on the table. Help your child count the interest. He will discover that he made a dollar just by keeping his money in savings.

Matching money saved Begin a matching programme. Create a further incentive. You, or maybe your child's grandparents, can pledge to 'match' any money she saves. Every two weeks, the 'matchers' and the child can sit down and count the total so she can see matching in action.

Put a plan in place Work together. You and your child should decide what portion of savings should go to short-term and long-term savings goals. Have your child draw or find a picture that illustrates a short-term goal, like a book or a toy. Another picture could show goals that are very far away, like a video game system or computer.

Family activity idea 8.4

Saving for a rainy day

Rain days can certainly put a damper on a visit to the beach or the park. They can also be great opportunities for quiet time – reading, playing cards, visiting a new website or finishing homework.

So when rainy days come, being prepared to adapt can make all the difference.

To help your child understand that sometimes things happen that we haven't counted on, read together and discuss the following books.

Three Little Pigs, any version (for ages 4 to 7)

Alexander, Who Used to be Rich Last Sunday by Judith Viorst (for ages 12 plus)

Alexander and the Terrible, Horrible, No Good, Very Bad Day by Judith Viorst (for ages 5 to 12)

A Chair for My Mother by Vera Williams (for ages 3 to 8)

The Three Sillies by Kathryn Hewitt (for ages 4 to 7)

Use these stories (and your own experiences) to emphasise that it's wise to expect the unexpected. You never know when you might lose your money, or the wolf might show up at your door, so be prepared!

Lesson 9

Laughing all the way to the bank

Big banks, little banks, piggy banks

Most parents don't keep their savings under the mattress because it won't grow anything but dust bunnies, and it's not safe. You can teach your children about saving and interest by visiting your local bank and opening a savings account. If your bank doesn't have a savings account specifically for children, ask about a no-fees, no-minimum-balance savings account instead.

Plant the seeds with a few dollars, and watch them grow into trees over the years. The amount of money in your child's savings account can grow quickly, even if they start small. Explain the complexity of interest with a simple example: the power of the dollar. If you put a dollar aside and doubled the amount every day, your money would grow rapidly. While the concept is far-fetched because banks don't pay 100 per cent interest, it is a useful example to show young children how money can grow, albeit rather more slowly.

In addition to teaching your children about interest, you can also teach them how to set and reach a savings goal. Remind them that if they take money out of their account early, there won't be as much to grow, so it won't grow as quickly. Finally, teach your children that saving money in the bank is safe – safer than keeping it in a piggy bank.

When do you open a savings account for your child?

Between eight and ten is ideal. Any earlier, and your child may be unwilling to part with her money. But by eight or so, your child is ready to understand how a bank works. Start by taking her to visit the bank. Some credit unions and banks cater well for children and will help explain how money is kept in a vault, how deposits are made and how money can be withdrawn. Show your child a bank statement to teach how savings accounts earn interest.

Many children get anxious when they learn that they won't get back the same notes and coins they are depositing. Explain that the bank keeps careful track of how much each person deposits, so she can always get that much out again. A savings account is the way to go at this age. Most are set up with a parent as the custodian, so at least initially your child will need to have you there to withdraw money.

Trips to the bank are a great opportunity to talk about saving. Decide together how much money will be kept at home for smaller purchases and agree to set a goal for the money in the savings account. Some parents even offer the incentive of matching what their child saves – maybe 50 cents for every dollar, or even dollar for dollar.

Once a child starts to receive an allowance and learn about money management, they are ready to open their own bank account. Many banks offer accounts especially tailored to teach children the basics of saving, investing and budgeting. These accounts tend to be free and pay interest. They can even include ATM cards, cheques, educational material, monthly or quarterly newsletters and online access.

Depending on the type of account, your child will most likely have to sign a signature card. This can be done in the bank itself or, if banking online, you can print out a signature card, have your child sign it, and mail it to the bank.

It's easy to set up transfers from a parent's to a child's bank account. For example, weekly allowances can automatically be transferred, eliminating the parent's need to search for cash and ensuring the commitment is honoured.

As you set up the bank account and weekly transfers, discuss the ground rules and any expectations for saving and spending. For example, if you also have a university fund set up, now is a great time to encourage saving a percentage for university. Not only does this make for a great excuse to write a cheque each month, but it also increases the child's ownership of their future education. And it teaches a fundamental saving rule: pay yourself first.

With online banking, it's tempting to simply set up a recurring transaction for something like monthly contributions to the university fund. There will be a time to teach that. For now, go with cheque writing. Writing out a cheque, entering it into the cheque book register, subtracting the amount from the balance and mailing the cheque are basic skills that the child should master before relying too heavily on the computer.

While automatic transfers into the account serve their purpose in making sure the allowance goes through, do let the child make some actual deposits from time to time. Birthday money, piggy-bank cash and money earned from chores are all great excuses to pull out a deposit slip and head to the bank.

Whether you give an allowance or make your child earn their own money, their first bank account is a rite of passage. Not only does it help instil a sense of responsibility when it comes to personal finances, it is also a great way to teach them about banking in general.

Getting your child his or her first bank account can help them become a responsible adult. Learning how to earn and save money for what they want will help them avoid debt and bad loans. Your child's first bank account is both educational and a sign of his growing up. Teaching children to become savers is an important lesson, and one that will pay big dividends down the road. Teach your children well and they will be the savvy investors of the future.

What types of accounts are available?

Choosing an account is the hardest part! There are many available, which can make narrowing it down to one very difficult. Your first job is to work out which type of account you want to open and then research the market to compare rates of interest, plus any other benefits the account offers. The best accounts for children tend to fall into one of the following categories.

Instant access accounts

These are flexible accounts that allow your child to withdraw money as and when she wishes. Most account holders will be issued with a card to withdraw money and just $1 is usually enough to get your child started! The interest rates can vary on accounts like these so you do need to be aware of interest changes taking place over time.

Fixed rate or term deposit accounts

If you want your child to save money over a long period, a fixed rate account can offer more security as your money will continue to grow at the same rate of interest in ten years as it did when you opened it. Some banks offer bonuses if you reach a certain amount, which is a good incentive for children to save as much as possible. You might also be given the option of having interest paid monthly or annually. The only downside to an account like this is general interest rates; if they rise during the fixed term you could see less of a return than other accounts, though this is generally deemed less of a risk by parents who want a secure return on their child's savings over the long term.

Trusts

If you want to invest money for your child but want to avoid shares, a trust or investment fund might be the best option. The idea with trusts is that your child's money is managed by somebody who invests it on their behalf. You can choose to build it up until your child reaches their teenage years, or sell your investments at any time, but beware of any set-up charges or annual running costs you may be liable for.

Bonus bonds

These offer a safe way to build savings with the added bonus of tax-free money prizes. For each $1 your child invests they will receive a series of numbers which could, if they're lucky, lead to a prize. Parents with children under 16 will need to buy the bonds on their behalf.

KiwiSaver

If you are in New Zealand, your children can join KiwiSaver. With no minimum age to join, the government incentives attached to KiwiSaver make it a great way to put money aside for your children's future. The funds will be locked in until age 65, but can be accessed earlier in certain circumstances, such as buying a first home. An early start works wonders (and $1000 on joining doesn't hurt either). KiwiSaver members under 18 can still receive the $1000 kick-start provided by the government. Once they turn 18 they may be eligible for tax credits matching the contributions made to their account, as well as other benefits such as withdrawing funds for their first home.

It's getting INT-eresting

Ahhh, the holy grail of bank accounts! Interest rates vary between banks, but if you shop around for an account that offers a high rate, your child can enjoy healthy boosts to their money as it grows. Many children's accounts offer higher interest rates than adult accounts, and since the rates change less regularly, there's less impact on the amount of interest your child receives over a period of time (though you do need to keep a close eye on rates as they can drop from time to time). It's also worth checking what your local building society has on offer, especially if you have an existing account there. Many building societies reserve special rates of interest for clients' children, so you might find a better deal there.

Some banks offer exceptionally high rates of interest, which can be a huge draw for parents searching for a good deal. Read the small print though, as it's likely the advertised rate has a limited shelf life, meaning your child's savings will quickly revert back to the bank's usual interest rate.

These basics of banking are important for your child to learn. They are tools they will use throughout their lives.

Family activity idea 9.1

Create an investing bank for money that will grow on its own

(and illustrate the difference between saving and investing)

The time factor

Investing is for a long time. Point out the difference between money that you save to spend pretty soon – or in a month or two – and money you save for a long time. The money that children save to buy a car or go to university will be saved for a very long time. People like to make that money grow over the years by earning interest, not sitting in a bank at home. The Growing bank helps children keep the money until there is enough to invest.

Growing money

First save a sizeable sum of money, say $20 or more (or whatever's age-appropriate). When you've reached your target, it's time to move money out of the Growing bank and into an investment where it will earn interest. Help your child remember what interest is by returning to the dollar and cents activity we discovered with the Saving bank.

Take a trip to the bank

Start with a bank deposit. If you put your money into a savings account, the money will be very safe, but it will earn only a little interest.

More risk

Explain to your child that there are other places to put money. For example, interest-bearing bonds, the share market or collectibles. Tell your child that investing in a place other than a savings account typically earns more interest than a savings account at the bank.

Which one's for you?

Pick an investment that fits your comfort level. Explain to your child which investment you are going to choose to help his or her money grow. Plus, explain how the investment works.

For older children

The concept of risk is really one for older children (it might make the younger ones nervous about the safety of their money). Many families start with cash funds backed by the government.

If you put your child's money in a non-guaranteed investment, like managed funds or shares, make an activity of tracking the money's progress: you and your child should watch the newspaper or the internet to see how the investment is doing.

If the investment dips, don't react in a way that will make the child anxious. Keep sending this message to your children: we leave money in an investment a very long time. The money will have its ups and downs, just as we have good days and bad days.

Decorate the bank

Stay focused. Decorate the bank with pictures of your child's long-term goal – a car, tertiary education or an overseas trip.

Family activity idea 9.2

Banks, bankers, banking and how they work

Step 1: Create the bank

Arrange the furniture in your lounge so that it simulates a bank lobby.

• Make sure there is a place for customers to line up.

• Use tables and chairs to make an area where the tellers help customers open their accounts.

• Make a bank vault. This will need to be in a safe place, possibly in the corner of the lounge. Make sure there is enough room to store everyone's deposit boxes.

Step 2: Hire the employees

• Mum or Dad is the bank manager. Choose soft toys, brothers, sisters or friends to work as tellers, guards, greeters and custodians. Some of the guards will bring money to the vault; others will keep the vault safe. Greeters will greet each customer as they enter and exit the bank. Custodians will keep the bank clean.

• What job would you most like to do? What do you need to know in order to be a good teller? What do the guards need to do? What would be the main role of a greeter? How important are custodians to the operation of a bank?

Step 3: Opening the accounts – customers

• Customers should decide how much money to put in the bank.

• Use a spare deposit slip from Mum or Dad's bank. Use this deposit slip to determine how much money you are going to deposit.

• When it is your turn, bring your money and your deposit slip to the teller.

• Remember, it is important to be polite. When you go to the teller, say: 'Hi, I would like to open an account please.'

• When the teller is ready, give her your money.

Step 4: Opening the accounts – tellers

• When a customer comes to you and tells you he or she wants to open an account, respond politely. Take the customer's deposit slip and look at the last name. Put Mr or Ms before the last name and call the customer by this name, as you do with your teacher. This shows respect. When a customer and a teller have a conversation, it's called a 'business relationship'. Politeness is important in business relationships.

When the customers give you their money, count it. When you are sure that you have counted correctly, check to see that the amount is the same as the amount the respective customers wrote on the deposit slips.

• Write the customer's name on a piece of paper. Then write your name and the amount deposited. This is called a deposit receipt. Give the deposit receipt to the customer.

Step 5: Guarding the money

• Each time a teller takes a deposit from a customer, a guard should bring the deposit box to the vault.

• At least two guards should be watching the vault at all times.

Step 6: Greeters and custodians

• Greeters must always be polite to customers. Greet them warmly as they enter and exit the bank. This can be done with a handshake or by a polite hello. Greeters must always try to make customers feel welcome in the bank.

• Custodians should use the props provided to clean the bank. It is important that the bank be clean in order for customers to feel welcome.

Conclusion

Banks play an important role in our society, and that means bank workers are important too! What job did you do? Did you understand your responsibilities? Did you enjoy it? Were you polite to the customers?

And customers, without you we wouldn't need banks. Did you understand how to open a bank account? Were you polite to the teller?

Family activity idea 9.3

What's my interest?

Explore the basics of earning interest by means of an interest-bearing jellybean account. Attain a basic understanding of the reasons banks pay interest, the value of saving and the effect that savings decisions can have on principal growth, and enhance a practical understanding of interest by making calculations of principal growth.

Distribute 15 jellybeans to each.

Each child has 15 jellybeans. This is your 'savings account'. You are free to 'spend' (in this case eat!) your jellybeans if you want. But wait – if you save them, you will earn more jellybeans.

Parents, inform the children of the interest rate and explain that the 'principal' is the original amount invested (and not the head of their school!). A suggested rate would be one jellybean added to each account for every five they have, per unit of time (compounding per hour would work well, in which case this activity would best be started at the beginning of the day). This rate will produce tangible increases that the child can easily perceive. Further calculations are not possible with jellybeans; thus, you will likely have to establish the rule that five jellybeans saved earns one in interest, but four or fewer will get nothing.

• How many will you save?

• How many will you eat?

• Write your answers down on a piece of paper. If you eat any throughout the day, make sure to write down how many.

Later, when your jellybean account has been growing all day, write answers to the following questions:

• How many jellybeans did you start with?

- How many did you eat?

- How many did you save?

- How many do you have now?

- Do you know how you got the number that you did?

- Based on the interest rate, how many will you have at the end of two days?

- How about at the end of the week?

- At the end of the month?

- What if you never eat any of your jellybeans?

Parents, assist your children to understand the interest rate and make their calculations. Don't forget about compounding (as interest is paid, it's added to the principal, and each future interest calculation is based upon that new, increased principal). What if you never eat any of your jellybeans? The principal will grow faster. However, money (or in this case, a jellybean) serves a purpose. Stimulate a brief discussion – does simple accumulation for its own sake make sense? Shouldn't some jellybeans be eaten/money be spent?

Lesson 10

Money makes the world go round

Using everyday opportunities to teach the value of money

Good money skills are learned, not inherited. The lessons you teach and the examples you set for your children early on will be the foundation of their future financial success.

Talking about money

When is it a good time to talk about money? You will have any number of great opportunities to talk to your children. All you have to do is to recognise them. And remember – you're talking, describing, explaining – not preaching.

Mealtimes

This should be when the family (or at least part of it) gathers and recaps their day. But many modern families have a hard time eating together because they are working around days filled with other activities, and money talks don't have to occur at home, with the whole family. Sometimes the best conversations begin spontaneously over hamburgers or pizza as you catch a meal on the way to somewhere else.

In the car

Whether or not your child has her driving licence, if you're like most families you're still spending a lot of time together in the car going here and there. Being shut in a vehicle together can provide just-you-and-me time. And conversation sure beats listening to the radio as your child surfs the music stations.

During quieter activities

No, you can't talk during a rugby match, but you could talk while you and your child clean out the garage, load the dishwasher, weed the garden or hang around a park with your dog. Granted, this is not the time for heavy-duty you'll-need-a-calculator-to-figure-out-the-savings talks, but you can easily deal with lighter, more casual topics.

Watching TV

Here's your big chance to play devil's advocate to the adverts that pelt your child's brain every ten minutes or so. And TV programmes often raise topics like saving and spending – they can portray a situation as either realistic or ridiculous. You can help teens make sense of what they see.

Shopping together

This is ideal as long as it doesn't end in an argument. Start when your children are younger and try to teach them about stretching their dollars, impulse purchasing, the hazards of credit, alternatives to brand slavery, shopping the sales, judging quality, recognising gimmicks and making good decisions. Again, this is colour commentary – an analysis of why you're purchasing, or not.

Paying bills

What better time to bring up the cost of living than when the stubs are staring you in the face? Put a few in a stack and do a little show-and-tell. Talk about what happens when you add them all up. You could get extreme and pile stacks of fives, tens and twenties on the kitchen table. Pay each bill by removing money from the stacks. It's a great exercise that makes a point visually and dramatically.

Our world is your classroom

When it's time to start passing on these valuable life lessons to your children, you can use the world around you as a financial classroom. Here are some ideas for doing so that you might like to make use of, adjusting of course for your child's age, experience and maturity.

Practice makes perfect

Put money into your children's awareness by constantly pointing it out in action. From the daily news to a trip to McDonald's, learning opportunities about money and its vocabulary are everywhere. Is the owner of the local fast-food place a franchisee? Who supplies them and how do they keep the food so consistent? Or, who invented Velcro or Post-it notes, and how did the inventor get the idea? To learn about shares, encourage your child to pick out companies they know, like Disney or Apple.

Application is doing

Nothing replaces the experiential lessons of doing. Taking the shares example further, buy shares in a publicly owned company and have your children track the investment. Children learn first-hand about profit and loss by taking a job, starting their own business or participating in school or group fundraising. We fail our children by over-protecting them. They need to learn from experience; confidence, self-esteem and lifelong skills come from success and failure alike. Celebrate the wins and don't concentrate on failures.

Family activity idea 10.1

Thinking about the role of money in everyday life

For many of us, money management can be a complicated matter, but the learning process of how to track and spend money doesn't have to be. There are several simple and practical exercises to get your young child thinking about the role of money in everyday life. Playing games, such as restaurant or grocery store, with your children to demonstrate how money is used is a good place to start.

Later on, reinforce what your child is likely already learning in school – differentiating among coins or using basic maths skills, for example. Try giving him a whimsical or mechanical bank to make saving money entertaining. A trip to the actual bank to see a teller and cash in the coins can become a monthly ritual for you and your child. This exercise will not only help him become familiar with saving, but also teach him a little bit about the bank and how deposits work.

Family activity idea 10.2

Financial learning experiences

You should look for opportunities to use common errands or outings with your children as financial learning experiences, such as figuring out the change owed after a purchase, or clipping coupons before you head to the grocery store.

Family activity idea 10.3

Going shopping

Going to the supermarket is often a child's first spending experience. About a third of our take-home pay is spent on grocery and household items. Spending smarter at the supermarket (using coupons, specials, sales and comparing unit prices) can save more than $1800 a year for a family of four. To help young people understand this lesson, demonstrate how to plan economical meals, avoid waste and use leftovers efficiently.

When you take children to other kinds of stores, explain how to plan purchases in advance and make unit/price comparisons. Show them how to check for value, quality, reparability, warranty and other consumer concerns.

Spending money can be fun and very productive when it's well-planned. Unplanned spending usually results in a percentage of our money being wasted because we get poor value.

Family activity idea 10.4

Using a credit card

When using a credit card at a restaurant, take the opportunity to teach children about how credit cards work. Explain to children how to verify the charges and how to guard against credit card fraud.

Family activity idea 10.5

Working for money

Money comes from work – not the ATM! Unless you come from a long line of super-wealthy people, you probably have to work for the money you get. It doesn't appear by magic out of a cash machine. However, for most children the experience is the opposite. They haven't had to work. All they need to do is ask. Children really benefit from understanding that Mum and Dad have to work hard for the money the family spends. Someday they will go to work to get their own money. Help them understand that doing well in school will help them get a better paying job.

As children get older, it is all right to exchange cash for extra work. Offer them opportunities to earn the money they need for the things they want. It isn't a good idea though to pay them to do things that they will have to do for nothing for the rest of their lives, like making their beds or cleaning up their rooms. It certainly won't hurt them to wash the car, clean out the garage or cut the grass for a little cash.

Lesson 11

'I want what I want'

Creating intelligent spenders

Take heed: spending is the key to savings, saving is the key to a prosperous financial future.

It's not just credit-based spending decisions that get people into trouble. Some people who have either exhausted their credit or ruined their credit rating have no trouble at all overspending. Cash slips through their fingers so fast that at the end of the day, if they started out with $50, they often have less than $5 remaining and will have great difficulty determining where it was all spent.

Does that sound familiar?

Practically everyone loves to spend money, surveys say, 'because it's fun'. Spending money is even more exciting, however, when it's carefully planned, because it will buy even more. But the advertising messages are irresistible – thousands, young and old, routinely take on expensive short-term credit card debt in addition to wasting a big percentage of their money because of poor spending practices.

Consider the extent to which some merchants and credit-card issuers will go in order to entice people to spend beyond their incomes: no-fee and low-fee credit cards, instant credit approvals, first-time buyer programmes, sweepstakes and competitions where chances of winning are increased with each credit-based purchase, extended manufacturers' warranty programmes, replacement insurance programmes and, of course, 'cash-back with every purchase'.

Family activity idea 11.1

Try this young spender's profile on your children

Spending Perception Scale

Listed below are 20 statements pertaining to spending techniques. There are five responses to select from, which indicate the degree to which you think the statement applies to you. Write the corresponding point number in the space at the end of the statement, then total up your points. Should a statement not apply to your situation, skip it and adjust the scoring accordingly.

Totally like me	1 point
A lot like me	2 points
Equally like and unlike me	3 points
A little like me	4 points

Not like me at all   5 points

	Score
1 Each time I receive any money, I usually put a small amount of cash aside as savings.	_____
2 Each time I receive any money, I usually deposit it into a cheque or savings account.	_____
3 I keep track of the money I receive from all sources.	_____
4 I set aside a predetermined portion of my money for regular weekly expenses.	_____
5 I set aside ten per cent of the money I receive for savings.	_____
6 My money (both spending and saving) is managed according to a written spending plan.	_____
7 My food and grocery spending is planned in advance and done with a list.	_____
8 I rarely make more than two trips a week to the dairy or supermarket.	_____
9 I use grocery and other coupons whenever possible.	_____
10 I do comparison shopping for quality, value, price, etc. for practically every purchase, large or small.	_____
11 I have no credit cards with a balance owing.	_____
12 I have no loans with a balance owing.	_____
13 I have comparison shopped for food and clothing in the last year.	_____
14 I do not dine out (breakfast, lunch or dinner) more than twice a week.	_____
15 I have received an earnings statement from Inland Revenue.	_____
16 I account for all my cash spending by collecting receipts.	_____
17 I balance cheque/savings accounts each time I receive a statement.	_____

	Score
18 I have looked into joining and/or am a member of a credit union.	_____
19 I am saving money towards my university education.	_____
20 I have given money/food to a needy person in the last two weeks.	_____

17–27	Very perceptive Time to teach others how to do it.
28–42	Pretty good Concentrate on improving a few of the weaker areas and you'll be amazed at the difference.
43–58	Average An hour a week focused on improving spending would increase savings and give you more to invest.
59–75	Lousy Immediate changes required to avoid financial disaster – implement a spending plan and get on a pay-as-you-go basis as soon as possible.
75+	It stinks! Contact a financial adviser for help or buy an appropriate book to help you improve your spending habits.

Source: Adapted from an idea by Paul Richard, Executive Director of the Institute of Consumer Financial Education, San Diego, USA.

How to develop improved spending: techniques and practices

• Write down all the poor spending practices that you want and need to change.

• Write down how you plan to implement the changes in each area.

• Construct a cashflow sheet showing income and outgoings.

- Set up and implement a spending plan.

- Discontinue borrowing and use of all credit cards.

- Begin collecting and making notes on your cash purchase receipts.

- Begin saving a dollar a day (or more), and all loose change.

- Look for alternatives and substitutes to spending.

- Start using supermarket coupons and send in for rebates.

- Wait for the sales. Comparison shopping can save more than 50 per cent.

- Take advantage of factory seconds, rebuilt and used items where practical.

- Start doing things for yourself that others were paid to do previously.

- Separate shopping trips (when comparing prices, value, reparability, etc.) from spending trips (when actually making the purchase).

- Avoid carrying credit cards, much cash or a cheque book on shopping trips.

The spending habits we instil in a child will have more impact on their financial life than any investment they may make in the future. I can't even begin to explain how critical it is for a child to have a clear grasp of this concept.

Ask yourself, have I set a good example? Have I taken the time to at least discuss the apparent lack of difference between a need and a want (as covered in Lesson 3)? To point out that your child's decisions now will define him as a person later on?

Remember these key messages:

1 Teach your children to delay the purchase and take time to think

An infant needs instant gratification. When he cries for a feed or because he hates the feeling of a soiled nappy, or when he wants a cuddle, parents act immediately. A child, on the other hand, has to start thinking about whether his desires need to be gratified instantly or not. Even a day or two to reflect will make a huge difference – relieving him of the pressure of the spending situation and teaching him to think about the difference between wants and needs.

2 Consider options and learn the art of being a thinking spender

A child learns best when she can see the options. What can she buy with her Christmas gift money? Help her to visualise and compare prices.

3 Help your children to think about long-term goals

Would it be better to save money and let it grow so something really significant can be bought in the future? Remember to teach compound interest and encourage your child to grow the money earned by investing it in a term deposit or managed fund.

4 Use supermarket trips to show your child how substituting works

Make the most of children wanting to help with grocery shopping. At a certain age, they just want to leave that chore to Mum and Dad. But while they still want to push the cart, incorporate a lesson on how substituting items can reduce the grocery bill.

5 Give children rewards when they save instead of spending

Double their savings or give them treats. Appreciate their efforts when they ask for an opportunity to earn money for prepay top-ups instead of asking for a loan. When they feel good about doing something, they stick with it longer.

Learning to spend

Let your child make mistakes

Learning to spend wisely involves a certain amount of trial and error. If you give your child an allowance but insist on approving all purchases, or if you give your child an advance every time she overspends, the financial planning lesson will be diluted.

So, lesson one for parents is 'hand over the money and try to keep your mouth shut'. (Of course, that doesn't apply if you have banned certain categories of toys from your home for reasons of principle.)

Here's an example. If little Jane immediately spends her entire weekly allowance on Barbie dolls, but three days later sees a colouring book she 'really wants', you shouldn't give in to her pleas for more money. In fact, you should rejoice because this is exactly the lesson you are trying to teach – when it comes to managing money, she needs to plan ahead.

Fortunately, Jane will learn this lesson when the consequences aren't too serious. Not having a colouring book at age seven is a lot more palatable than not being able to repay $10,000 in credit card debt at 27.

Fun with comparison shopping

If you talk to your children about comparison shopping, you might be surprised at how interested they are. Lots of children are fascinated by details and will gladly search the supermarket aisles for the cheapest package of rice.

To illustrate the lesson, you could try paying them the difference between a more expensive package and the one on special they find for you. These discounts are noted on the receipt, providing an excellent visual lesson in the merits of spending wisely.

Adults in general aren't very good role models. In much of the developed world, thrift has become unfashionable. Household saving rates in OECD countries have fallen sharply in recent years. English-speaking countries – the US, Canada, the UK, Australia and New Zealand – have the lowest rates of household saving. In Australia and New Zealand personal saving rates are negative as people borrow to consume more than they earn.

If you want to help your children form habits that may save them from amassing debt as adults, you need to help them practise delaying gratification. You can put them on the right track by encouraging them to save a certain amount each week towards a realistic goal.

Saving is a habit. Once children get into the habit, they don't miss the money. It's like contributing to a retirement plan. What's more, it's hard to beat the exhilaration that comes with buying something you've saved for. With your retirement plan, your savings goal is a happy retirement. Your child's savings goal could be a special toy or book, a bike or a computer.

To help your child set realistic goals, you should discuss what she wants to buy, find out the price and figure out how much she'll have to save each week to buy it by a certain date. Your child might want to have both short-term and long-term savings goals.

Visual aids are useful. For younger children, you could cut out a picture of the desired item and tape it onto a glass jar. Every week as the child puts more money in the jar she literally sees the money grow toward her objective. An older child could keep track of savings in a register, and redo the calculations each week.

You might consider contributing some money, too, if it is a big purchase, as long as the money is used specifically for that item. Think of it as your 'parental match' on your child's retirement plan!

You might find the following activities useful.

Self-control

Self-control is an important skill for children to learn. It refers to having power or control over one's own actions. It also means that an individual knows right from wrong. Children who rely on other children, parents, teachers or adults to make behavioural choices for them don't learn self-control. These children may follow others' poor choices and get involved in bullying, stealing and generally failing to take responsibility for the consequences of their behaviour.

Family activity idea 11.2

Create a spending bank for money to be used soon

Making a wish list

Children want so many things, but help your child think through what is reasonable and what he or she can afford. Making a wish list helps children stay focused. Next, approximate the price of what is on the list.

They can't have it all

Understand that some items are more important than others. Explain to your child why he or she can't buy everything on the wish list at once. Here's a chance to talk about basic concepts in money management:

- making choices

- evaluating cost – what's affordable or reasonable

- weighing trade-offs in a purchase decision

- delaying purchases

- opportunity cost – when you buy one thing, you forgo something else

Work with your child to rank the items on the wish list. Help them go over the list every few weeks to see if new things should be added, old ones dropped or items moved up or down the list.

Let them become wise consumers

Look for good deals. Before a purchase, help your child 'price shop'. Compare prices from store to store. Or scout out prices in newspaper ads or on the internet. Teach your child the value of doing pricing homework before spending.

Stretching your dollars

Count up the savings. If your child is able to buy an item on sale or find a better price at one store than another, count up the money saved. Drop the saved money in the Spend bank and talk about how that money is already giving your child a head start toward saving for the next item on the wish list.

Decorate the bank

Stay focused. Cut out or draw pictures of the first item on your child's wish list.

Family activity idea 11.3

Spending goals worksheet

I'm accumulating for the next .... months for the following goal(s):

Draw or stick pictures
of your goal(s) here

A description of my goal(s):

My goal(s) will cost: $ ....

Children may also imitate others in saying negative things about people who are different due to skin colour, race, culture, religion or disabilities. The skill of self-control will help children to grasp that tolerance of others is the right course. If students are taught self-control at an early age, they will feel better about the choices they do make.

General strategies for teaching self-control

It is important to select age-appropriate goals for children who are learning self-control. Try simple goals first, where success can be expected one goal at a time.

For preschool children, appropriate goals might include not interrupting or fighting with siblings. For early primary-age children, appropriate goals might include complying with bedtime rules or showing anger appropriately (instead of hitting or screaming). Some strategies that may help children learn appropriate self-control behaviours include:

Taking a break Encourage children to take a break or time out from a situation where they are feeling angry or upset.

Provide attention Children can learn to resist the temptation to interrupt if they're taught to observe when others are not talking, giving them an opportunity to join in appropriately. Providing children with attention at certain times makes them less likely to interrupt at the wrong time.

Use appropriate rewards Children need consistent, positive feedback to learn appropriate behaviour. Praise and attention are highly rewarding for young children, as is special time with a parent. Be sure your child knows what behaviour is desired!

Use specific activities designed to teach self-regulation Parents can help teach skills that foster self-control even to children as young as five to eight years. At the end of this chapter there are some activities to get you started. These skills include dealing with wanting what they can't have, understanding feelings and controlling anger.

Dealing with wanting what they can't have

Young children can become quite upset when their needs, or wishes, aren't met immediately. Often they don't know how to handle their frustration when told 'no' or 'later' by a parent or guardian. Similarly, young children often don't understand when a particular child has restrictions placed on him because of his family's beliefs or cultural background. In order to have positive experiences at home, at school and in the community, children need to learn skills to handle these feelings appropriately.

Teach children to use the following steps (see the puppet activity over the page):

1. SAY, 'I would like to (have) _____ but I can't right now.'

2. THINK about your choices:

- ask again later

- find something else to do

- ask to borrow it

- ask to share it

- ask about doing chores to earn money to buy my own _____

- wait my turn

- accept that I'm not allowed ('I would like it, but that's okay').

3. ACT out your best choice.

Family activity idea 11.4

Puppet role-playing activity

This activity will help your child learn to identify a particular thing she wants and cannot have. She'll learn to talk about the feelings associated with not being able to have it and review the choices she has in dealing with the situation.

Materials Paper, crayons or felts, puppets.

Directions

1 Ask your child to write about or draw a picture of a thing or activity she wishes she had or could do.

2 Have a conversation with your child about what she wishes or wants, and why.

3 Tell your child about something you wish you could have or do, and why.

4 Use puppets to play different roles in the following pretend situations:

• Your friend has a new toy that you've been wanting for weeks.

• You want to play with your friend, but he has to spend the day with his family.

• A girl you know who uses a wheelchair has a computer game you love to play.

• Your brother got a great cricket set for his birthday – just like the one you want.

Ideas for discussion during role playing

Use these questions to help your child think through appropriate choices and behaviours in the role-plays above:

• How do you feel when you see another child with what you'd like to have?

• How would it feel if someone took one of your toys without your permission?

• What can we do when we want someone else's things? What are our choices?

• What can we do when someone else gets to do what we want to do? What are our choices?

Family activity idea 11.5

Halt-Plot-Do-Review

Halt

Stop and ask yourself, Do I really want to spend money on this? If you're pretty sure you do, can you think of three reasons why?

[Space left intentionally blank in original book]

Plot

What will I have to give up if I spend money on this? In other words, what goods and services will I not be able to buy if I choose to spend on this?

Is there a substitute, say a different brand, that I might want more or that might cost less?

Is there anything that bothers me about buying this _____?

[Space left intentionally blank in original book]

Do

Go for it! Buy those new jeans, save for those rollerblades, go to that movie – or choose not to!

Review

How did it go? Am I satisfied with my spending decision?

Did I have to give up something else because of my spending decision?

Would I make the same decision again?

Family activity idea 11.6

Supermarket coupons – your money or your time?

Here are some tips to help your child take charge of savings coupons:

1 As an incentive, allow your child to keep the savings from the coupons used (or you can split the savings).

2 The child must be responsible for clipping, organising and shopping with the coupons. You may want to provide a special pair of scissors, envelopes and a container to help with this task.

3 Encourage your child to match coupons with the items on your shopping list prior to going to the store. This will minimise time spend in aisles thumbing through coupons.

4 Try not to let your child pressure you into purchasing items and/or brands you wouldn't normally buy. You might agree to try one new product each shopping trip. Remember, savings aren't really savings if you end up throwing the product away.

5 Save a month's worth of cash register receipts in a box. Ask your child to calculate total coupon savings for a month. You might also have your child calculate the new price of each item after a coupon is used. You can even encourage him to keep a record of the prices of a frequently used family product like toothpaste – with a coupon, without a coupon, on sale, at a discount store versus a grocery store, and so on – to help with comparison shopping.

6 Either on a weekly or monthly basis, pay the child the amount saved or the split amount to which you have agreed.

Lesson 12

Let the buyer beware!

The cure for affluenza

You're out mowing your lawn one day and you happen to glance up from your beat-up old mower at the house across the street where your neighbour is pulling into his driveway in a brand-new Lexus while a team of hired gardeners manicure his lush green lawns. You don't get it. His house is similar to yours and you know he and his wife aren't earning megabucks. How does he have so many more toys than you? How can he afford them?

Well, rest easy my hard-working friend; like so many other people in Western countries, he can't. He's just another victim of the endless pursuit of bigger and better material possessions, regardless of whether he can afford them or not. Sure, a brief surge of envy might wash over you, but it'll pass. Resist the urge to keep up with the Joneses; you'll be happy you did.

Why do we do it?

We are nothing if not great spenders. Status symbol envy runs rampant and today's advertising tells you everything is within your financial reach. With instant loans and credit cards freely available, we believe it too. But spending heedlessly without cash resources to back up the habit is putting us in bigger and bigger financial holes. So why do we do it?

First, we work hard. Many spend hours every day commuting to unsatisfying jobs. Spending helps to release the stress of the everyday grind and at the same time seems to justify the slavery of our jobs.

And television has made us believe that high-end items like BMWs and Tag Heuer watches are to be had by everyday working stiffs, not just the super-rich.

But what really drives our ultra-spending is our own insecurity. Though it's a fact that everybody struggles from time to time, we'd all like to look as if we've made it financially – we can afford the luxuries of life. This is just the start of a vicious cycle.

We want to reassure ourselves that our material goods are on a par with or better than anything our peers have. We don't stop to think about the poor and the homeless, to count our financial blessings. The endless quest for bigger and better toys makes us lose sight of what's really important in life. In the meantime, we bury ourselves under a heap of debt from which we'll be hard-pressed ever to emerge.

Warding off affluenza

Flu season comes around every year, but social analysts worry about another virus that's usually at its height around Christmas. It's called affluenza.

Authorities describe affluenza as an unearned feeling of entitlement for luxuries, and it's becoming an epidemic, especially among children. The primary symptom is overconsumption. John de Graaf, David Wann and Thomas H. Naylor, authors of *Affluenza: The All-Consuming Epidemic,* describe affluenza as:

- a fever for shopping and spending

- swollen expectations over material needs

- decreasing immunity to the assaults of advertisers

- self-concepts defined by brands of clothing

- a rash of debt by the time the victims leave tertiary institutions.

Like ordinary flu, affluenza can be a minor inconvenience or a dangerous infection. In many cases it manifests itself in a whiny, selfish child with an overdeveloped sense of entitlement. And sometimes that child grows into a self-indulgent adult looking for a free ride through life. Fortunately, if it's caught early, affluenza can be cured.

The disease

Children often define their identity through possessions, and these items become more important than relationships. This attitude progresses with the accumulation of more material goods as years go by.

Childhood affluenza is not based on wealth. It's based on the values learned while growing up. When children from wealthy households are infected, the presence of the money becomes a disincentive for them to lead productive lives. Even when the family is far from affluent, children want and expect everything they see advertised.

The cause

Scientists point to two primary causes: omnipresent marketing, and parents who spoil their children. They fret over children's exposure to advertising. Children are bombarded from the time they get up until they go to bed. The primary message is that acquiring things will make you happy.

Children are exposed to as many as 40,000 advertisements a year. Affluenza is an airwave-borne epidemic. The average 12-year-old child spends 48 hours a week exposed to commercial messages, and only one and a half hours in significant conversation with her parents.

Teenagers are also getting messages from Hollywood, the place they look to for the latest trends. And they're not just reading about extravagant lifestyles. Their attitudes are warped by reality shows like *The Simple Life* on E! and MTV's *My Super Sweet 16.*

The Simple Life chronicled the adventures of Paris Hilton and Nicole Richie, daughter of singer Lionel Richie, when they took on low-paying jobs while deprived of their accustomed luxuries. *My Super Sweet 16* documents rich children marking their 16th birthdays with flamboyant celebrations.

Research has shown that children in Guatemalan refugee camps and those in landless peasant settlements in Brazil appear cheerful and resourceful despite an almost total lack of possessions, while their affluent counterparts in developed countries are submerged in goods but feel deprived.

Children's exposure, not only to ads but also to peer pressure, offsets parental modelling. Many parents aren't making it clear enough to children that they don't need everything that's advertised. Wealthy parents face a challenge because there are fewer limits to what they can buy, while less affluent families have more realistic limits. But in many instances, parents use gifts as a substitute for something that's priceless: time. Many parents work long hours and some shower their children with gifts instead of being physically present – chequebook parenting.

Treatment and prevention

Although it might seem like the symptoms are incurable, childhood affluenza can be remedied. Begin by attacking the bug with a dose of communication and corrective action to prevent you and your child from overindulging. Don't let your children get away with nagging. Let them figure out for themselves what they can do to relieve boredom.

Put strict limits on their television viewing and set up frequent opportunities for meaningful one-on-one time with your child. Explain that you want to make some positive changes in the way the family is living. Don't just discuss what you're planning to take from them. Phrases like 'more balance', 'a simpler life', 'fewer but cooler things' can figure in the discussion.

Recession and reassurance

I spoke to some of my friends with children and asked if the financial crisis featured in their social studies or economics classes. 'Not really,' they said.

With all due respect to their children's teachers, it seems to me they're passing up a prime teachable moment – certainly for highschool and university students. An opportunity missed, surely, to talk to kids about how we got into this situation and how we might get out of it.

What younger children crave most is reassurance. Here are six ways parents can provide it:

1. **Remember that little pitchers really do have big ears** Even if you don't discuss your financial situation with children directly, they can sense that something is up if you're worried about your finances or that you might lose your job. If you ignore the situation, children may imagine it's worse than it really is.

2. **Children live in a black-and-white world** They take you literally. Don't resort to black humour about going broke or ending up in the poorhouse. They may not know what a poorhouse is, but they'll figure it can't be good.

3. **Turn off the TV and tune out the talking heads** It's one thing to be well informed, but exposing your children (and yourself) to a steady stream of hyped-up headlines and downbeat news is bad for the psyche.

4. **A little honesty goes a long way** Children don't want or need to know all the details of your balance sheet. They just want to know that, hard times or no, they will have a roof over their heads and food on the table and that things will get better.

5. **Have a plan** If you've lost your job, for example, or anticipate that you might, tell the children how you'll go about looking for a new

one. Meanwhile, let them know that you'll be able to collect unemployment benefits, or that your spouse or partner will bump up his hours to tide you over.

6. **Encourage children to help out** Let them know that their holiday wish lists will have to be shorter this year. They'll be happy to do their bit for the family. And look on the bright side: this may be your chance to think creatively about cutting back on holiday overload and put affluenza in its place, a desirable goal even without a fiscal crisis.

Protect your children with sound financial advice

If you don't have conversations about balancing a cheque account, choosing a credit card, how to save – basic financial management – with your children, you're allowing *My Super Sweet 16* to teach your children about finances.

Television is the hot zone for affluenza. Children should be taught media literacy to help protect them against manipulation. Parents should also use their influence to reduce advertising received at their children's schools.

Banks and financial consultants offer counselling services that advocate honesty and philanthropy to children. The consultants also suggest getting children involved with a family's charitable foundation and/or other organisations that help those in need. Philanthropy can not only highlight the family's values and legacy, but also develop financial and life skills.

For older children, especially if your family is one with financial resources, set up family meetings. These meetings promote one-on-one time and discussions about the family's financial business and philanthropic decisions. They can also include a financial adviser to help support financial education, as well as fun events such as a family holiday.

Once again, though, parents should set the standard by demonstrating moderation.

Affluenza among the super-rich

We're seeing the largest transfer of wealth the developed world has ever experienced. According to research by Cap Gemini/Ernst and Young, the next decade will see over a trillion dollars transferred from one generation of wealthy to the next. For those on the giving and the receiving ends of that transfer, it's a mixed blessing.

While wealthy parents generally take pride in their ability to provide well for their children, the sheer size of some estates brings up difficult questions. Will these children be able to manage their money wisely? Will a large inheritance enrich their lives? Or will it turn them into underachievers? When it comes to inheritance, how much is too much?

A growing concern

Awareness of this issue is a start, but it doesn't necessarily mean action. Part of the problem is that affluenza is as much about family relationships as it is about money. Parents may talk about estate planning from a 'tax-efficiency' perspective, but they won't go a step further to involve the beneficiaries, i.e. their children, in that process. The children end up with the inheritance, but they're not prepared for it. So the money goes into an ill-conceived business venture, or it's lost through poor investment or frivolous activity.

Family matters

The source of affluenza is not in the estate plan, but in the difficult relationships some wealthy families have with money. Many entrepreneurs are so wrapped up in their businesses that the only real connection they have with their children is buying them whatever they want.

But no two families will experience affluenza in quite the same way. It's not always about trying to make young wealthy individuals understand the value of their parents' wealth. It can just as easily be about parents trying to make sure family money stays in the family. A large inheritance can be a disruptive influence on an heir's relationships and the cause of ongoing conflict. And if any part of the inheritance is used for family purposes, it could be at risk of becoming a family asset and therefore subject to division upon dissolution of the heir's marriage. By bequeathing assets to a trust, rather than to children directly, the wealthy hope to prevent a big inheritance from becoming an issue in relationship breakdown.

For other wealthy individuals, the issue is how to protect children against the temptations of wealth. One solution is an 'incremental inheritance' – gradual payment of the inheritance as the child reaches certain milestones. Such an arrangement can go a long way toward ensuring the child doesn't fall victim to the 'dark side' of wealth.

Lesson 13

The hot stove principle

Teaching a healthy fear of debt

One of a parent's major responsibilities to their children is to make sure they're ready to enter the adult world when they leave the nest. This should include financial know-how, but unfortunately most parents don't talk to their children about credit and debt until it's too late. If a child is old enough to make and spend money, he's old enough to understand the basics of good credit and its importance.

Most children receive some form of allowance from their parents. If this is an option you choose, you're helping your child take the first steps to good credit-management. Teaching your child the basics of budgeting, such as how to balance a cheque book, at an appropriate age, and helping your child open a savings account are also steps in the right direction. Even if the bank account never gets into triple figures, it still teaches your child the importance of saving for the future.

Credit cards are difficult for most children to manage, so only in rare cases should a teen be allowed to have one. Paying your child's credit card bills or other debts leads to irresponsible misuse of these tools, which can damage them greatly in the future. Good credit is only possible for adults who are responsible with their money. Rather than allowing her to have a credit card, encourage your child to speak with you if she really does need money in advance, and be open to her ideas.

But you can help your child build future credit by putting one of your own bills in his name. A small utility bill is a good option. Your child does not actually need to pay this bill; it's simply a way for him to build good credit. Since you have to pay the bill monthly, it doesn't make any difference whose name it's in. You can get your child involved by having him remind you when the bill is due and keeping a record of the payments. This teaches good habits, and getting into the habit of maintaining good credit is the most important thing at this stage.

The discipline line

The word discipline has negative connotations involving authority and punishment. A more constructive concept is 'positive discipline'.

Positive discipline is all about creating an orderly environment where people can conduct themselves according to agreed standards of behaviour for everyone's benefit. In this way we can avoid unnecessary conflict and potential accidents.

Most family groups establish an atmosphere of positive discipline, which protects individuals' rights but also encourages harmony. Positive discipline is also an excellent learning medium for our children, allowing them to develop in a safe environment.

Negative discipline is damaging to group harmony. Potential for a negative discipline situation occurs when rules are disobeyed or when they are clearly accepted reluctantly.

The first step is to establish and maintain a reasonable, but firm, discipline line. When the line is too high, or restrictive, children feel resentment and they don't listen. Too low or liberal, and children take liberties. Once again, they don't listen.

This line must be a well-defined set of behaviour standards that you expect your children to abide by and support. It's also important to ensure that these standards, or rules, are communicated clearly and everyone is fully aware of them. This will ensure your children know what's expected and what's not permitted.

It is essential to set a discipline line that is achievable and effective in the real world. The key success factors are:

- consistency
- clear communication
- fairness

- flexibility

- immediacy.

There are many aspects to positive discipline and the following is an interesting one.

The 'hot stove rule'

However well you handle discipline, it remains an unpleasant task that often causes resentment. The challenge is to apply the disciplinary action necessary to create a healthy fear of debt in your children.

An effective way to incorporate the principles described above is to adopt the hot stove rule. The consequences of touching a hot stove are immediate; there's no doubt about the cause and effect. Everyone knows what happens if you touch a hot stove, so advance communication is not an issue, and the results are consistently painful. They can also be seen as impersonal – anyone touching a hot stove is going to get burnt. So discipline is directed against the act, and not the individual. The comparison between debt and the hot stove rule is obvious.

Credit cards

Credit cards can teach children how to manage and establish credit records, which will be helpful later in life when they want to buy a home. Credit cards also teach financial responsibility; however, some parents think giving a child a credit card is a straight shot into debt.

As you probably know, credit card companies have for some time aimed heavy marketing at young people in tertiary institutions. These companies are moving on now to even younger and less responsible consumers, focusing on high school students. Research has told them teens are working and spending their own earnings along with money from their parents, so it's no surprise co-signed credit cards are being marketed to high school children. The offers they get through the mail allow credit limits as low as $200. Granted, the cards offer parents low-level protection, but they also come with high interest rates. And since parents co-sign, they are legally responsible for the account.

Debit cards

Another option for teens and parents to consider is prepaid, or debit, cards. Parents apply for a card in the child's name and deposit money in the account. The prepaid cards are able to be used anywhere Visa or MasterCard are accepted. They also come with extra features like online account control and tools, financial lessons and interactive games designed to teach fiscal responsibility.

Parents can track what the child is spending money on, and have the option to reload the account when it's low. Debit cards are good for teens because they can't overspend the account and accumulate finance charges, other fees and overall debt.

Handling your child's use of credit or debit cards

Whichever option you choose when teaching your child financial responsibility, there are a few guidelines to consider.

- Be clear about what your child can and can't use the card for.

- Teach children to use their credit card only for things they would be willing to pay for with cash.

- Track transactions and balances in the register and don't forget to include debit card or ATM fees.

- Collect all sales receipts to prevent a thief using the information to make purchases.

- Go over monthly statements with your children and monitor their spending habits.

- Sit down with your children and show them what fees and interest can cost over time.

Family activity idea 13.1

How do credit cards work?

This simulation requires three people (children and parents) for the roles of Consumer Mum (or Dad), Sammy (owner of Shoes-Are-You store), and Banker Bonnie (or Craig), a banker at the card-issuing bank.

The following materials are needed for the simulation.

- two or three Monopoly $1 notes
- ten x20-cent pieces
- copy of playing cards, cut apart
- empty wallet
- a bank credit card
- one shoe
- calculator or toy machine
- envelope addressed to Consumer Mum (or Dad)
- envelope addressed to bank (issuer of credit card)
- copy of 'What's Up?'

To conduct the simulation:

1 Deal playing cards to the people indicated on each card.

2 All money (banknotes and 20-cent pieces) should be with Banker Bonnie (or Craig).

3 Sammy should have one shoe on display.

4 The envelope addressed to Consumer Mum goes to the bank; the envelope addressed to the bank goes to Mum.

5 Mum, Dad, an adult or older child should read the scenarios and directions on 'What's Up?'

Playing cards

1 Bank's money Deal face up to the banker, and stack two or three $1 notes and four 20-cent pieces on the card	**2** Consumer Mum's bank account money Deal face up to the banker, and stack six 20-cent pieces on the card
3 Credit card record Consumer Mum bought one shoe for $1 Deal face down to Sammy at Shoes-Are-You	**4** Credit card receipt Consumer Mum bought one shoe for $1 Stick in shoe at shoe store
5 Credit card bill You owe $1 for the shoe you bought: pay now $1.00, pay later $1.20 Deal face down to Banker Bonnie/Craig	**6** A cheque for $1 from Mum to the bank A cheque tells the bank to take the money out of your account to pay for something you bought Deal face down to Consumer Mum

What's Up?

Mum, Dad or an older child should read aloud the following transactions as Mum uses her credit card.

1 Consumer Mum wants to buy one shoe from Shoes-Are-You. She needs $1 to pay for the shoe, but her wallet is empty. All she has is a shiny credit card from _____ (use name of bank issuing credit card, which may be on the front or back of the card). Can Mum use the card to buy the shoe? (Mum waves the credit card.)

2 Consumer Mum shows the credit card to Sammy, owner of the Shoes-Are-You store. 'Yes,' Sammy says to Consumer Mum, 'you can use that credit card to buy this shoe.'

3 Sammy takes the credit card from Mum and swipes it through the credit-card machine (use calculator or toy machine). Sammy returns the credit card to Mum and gives her the shoe with the Credit Card Receipt (Card #4) sticking out of the shoe.

4 Consumer Mum reads the Credit Card Receipt aloud: 'Consumer Mum bought one shoe for $1.' Mum puts the credit card and the receipt into her wallet. She will need the receipt if she returns the shoe, and to compare with the bill that will come from the bank.

5 Sammy now turns over and reads aloud the Credit Card Record (Card #3): 'Consumer Mum bought one shoe for $1.' Sammy presents this card to Banker Bonnie/Craig at the _____ (bank that issued the credit card).

6 Banker Bonnie/Craig takes the Credit Card Record (Card #3) from Sammy and gives him/her a $1 bill from the notes labelled 'Bank's Money' in exchange.

7 Sammy is happy. He/she has sold a shoe for $1 (Sammy waves dollar note). Consumer Mum is happy. She has a new shoe (Mum waves shoe). Banker Bonnie is happy. She has 'loaned' $1 of the bank's money to Consumer Mum to buy a shoe (Banker Bonnie/Craig waves Credit Card Record).

8 Has Consumer Mum paid for the shoe yet? (No. When she used her credit card to buy the shoe, she was promising to pay in the future.

Sammy gave Mum's 'promise-to-pay' to the bank, and the bank paid for the shoe. Now, Mum owes $1 to the bank.)

9 Banker Bonnie turns over the Credit Card Bill (Card #5) and reads it aloud. The banker then puts the bill (Card #5) into the envelope addressed to Mum and 'delivers' it to her.

10 Consumer Mum opens the bill and reads aloud her choices: 'You owe $1 for the shoe you bought: pay now $1, pay later $1.20.' What should Mum do?

11 Consumer Mum now turns over Card #6, a cheque for $1 from Mum to the bank, and reads it aloud. Mum has decided to pay $1 now instead of paying $1.20 later. She puts the cheque (Card #6) into an envelope addressed to the bank and 'delivers' it.

12 Banker Bonnie opens the envelope from Consumer Mum. The Banker reads aloud again from Card #6: 'A cheque tells the bank to take the money out of your account to pay for something you bought.' Banker Bonnie moves five x20-cent pieces from the card labelled 'Consumer Mum's Money' over to the card labelled 'Bank's Money'.

The transaction is complete! Mum is happy; she has paid for a new shoe (Mum waves shoe). Sammy is happy; he/she has sold a shoe for $1 (Sammy waves $1). Banker Bonnie is happy because Consumer Mum has paid her credit card bill and is using credit wisely (Banker holds up five x20 cent pieces).

Extension questions

• Suppose Mum didn't have $1 in the bank when the credit card bill came? She would have to pay $1.20 to the bank later when she had the money.

• What if Mum made a mistake and sent the cheque for $1 to the bank when there wasn't enough money in her bank account? The bank would send the cheque back to Mum marked 'Insufficient funds'. She would have to write another cheque for $1.20 later when she had money in her bank account. And the bank would charge her a fee (more money) for 'bouncing' a cheque.

Lesson 14

Sharing is caring

Moving children beyond the 'me' stage

When you are around a gaggle of two- and three-year-olds, it doesn't take long to figure out one of the challenges for that age group is sharing. Just when you're figuring out that you have a separate identity of your own, it must be quite a tall order to be asked to consider others.

Sometimes it seems we need constant reminders of the lessons we were supposed to absorb at an early age. It's so easy to get distracted by our busy lives and forget our responsibilities to others. However, the fact remains that it is our duty, as parents, to teach our children to share. This means that we should role-model, facilitate, encourage and celebrate sharing and community service.

To start with, some ideas for doing this with your children include:

- discuss why sharing is important

- discuss how sharing with others makes you feel

- discuss how it feels to have others share with you

- discuss how it would feel not to have things you need (food, a home, love, clothes)

- provide your children with opportunities to discover ways they can share what they have

- encourage giving to others by setting aside money, time or resources for your child to give to causes of their choice.

Part of a solid money education includes teaching your children that, as a member of a community and a citizen of the world, they have a responsibility to other people outside themselves and their family. That means sharing. We all live on a small planet together, and we are all linked. Teaching your children a sense of social ethics includes an awareness of the importance of charity or giving.

The time to introduce them to charity is around three to four. Until then, children don't understand that other people have different ideas and feelings.

Young children first learn the concept of sharing when they exchange or share toys. Sharing develops thoughtfulness and generosity. Encourage children to give to community charity projects by donating money or gently-used toys, books and clothing. This develops a concern for others by going beyond the family circle. Some parents expect a certain percentage of the allowance to be given to others.

In addition to teaching children to share, this exposes them to the satisfaction that comes from helping others. Decide as a family how often you'll pass on usable things in good shape that you no longer need.

Make it a scheduled family event. Once every month or two, decide what you might like to pass on to a charity. Let the children have a say in what they want to donate. Another idea is to keep a box labelled for donations available to add things to as you come across them. When the box is full, take it to the charity. You can even arrange for it to be picked up, as many charities will collect contributions.

If you have the opportunity to give to a specific charitable organisation, explain to your son or daughter there are many children who don't get Christmas presents. Get your child involved, take her to the toy store to pick out a gift, have her help wrap it and finally accompany you when you donate it. Children look up to their parents and learn by example.

Donating time is also a great way to help. Maybe the charity needs help at a fundraiser or contributions for a cake stall. If everyone donates a little time, far more gets done. Many children's charities support children who have to spend a lot of time in hospital. Taking the time to make their stay more pleasant can be a great way to help a children's charity. One way to help is by visiting and helping to brighten up the children's wards with artwork.

There are many charities out there, but it is important to research before you donate. Unfortunately, there are people who will take advantage of others' generosity. If you stick with the better known charities, such as the Make-a-Wish Foundation, Ronald McDonald House or UNICEF, you'll be certain of helping a truly worthy cause.

There are also local children's charities and programmes that are equally respected. If you need ideas, talk to your local children's hospital. They can probably give you a list of organisations looking for donations or volunteers. Some hospitals have book or toy collections where you can drop off your donations. Check with the local religious community, as they may have ties to special children's charities.

Helping others is a great way to give back a little of what we've received. It helps us to keep a perspective on what is important in life. It helps others to have a better life, and it helps your child to realise at an early age the value of giving to others who are less fortunate.

You can help your child develop a sense of social responsibility in the following ways:

• Start small when the children are small

Your young child might be happy to help bake cookies for a friend but end up wanting to keep the gift herself. Plan for this by baking enough cookies to keep as well as give. Young children need help in learning to share.

• Teach them how to give

Talk with them about how you decide what to give and where. Teach them to evaluate which causes are worthy and to balance giving with saving and spending. This is better than simply telling them they should be generous without offering any guidelines.

• Teach your child that he or she doesn't need money to give

Help your child make gift certificates good for 'one free car wash' or 'breakfast in bed' that she can give to others in the family.

• Be a role model

Volunteer your family's time at a soup kitchen or retirement home. Gather small toiletries like toothpaste and shampoo, and pack them in decorated gift bags to take to a homeless shelter. Ask your child if he'll help you baby-sit a neighbour's toddler so she can do her shopping, or help you rake the leaves for an elderly friend.

• Share your work speciality with others who can't afford it

This is an option for people who are knowledge or service 'rich' but cash 'poor'. Donate your services to a worthy cause of your choice, and bring your children along with you. They'll learn a valuable lesson as you participate in improving the world.

• Volunteer together

Generosity doesn't always mean financial giving. Helping others, whether by volunteering through a non-profit organisation or through personal acts of kindness, is a generous act. Volunteering helps children see that others have needs they can help fill and encourages them to think more about others and less about themselves.

• Engourage individual participation

Stress to your child that it's not enough that the family gives – each individual needs to participate, too.

• Give

It's not about how much you give. Every little bit helps.

• Involve your child in selecting the gift

You may think that donating to cancer research is important, but your child who is an animal lover may be more interested in making sure the dogs at the humane society have an extra treat at the holidays. Help her find a way to give the gift she feels is important.

• Designate a portion of their allowance to give away

One of the best methods is the glass jar system. Let your children decide how to spend the 'for giving' money, so long as they don't spend it on themselves.

• Help a child who is the same age as your own

At Christmas, choose an angel from a charity tree and let your child select the gift to buy.

Alternatively, extend the giving throughout the year by sponsoring a child through Compassion, World Vision or a similar organisation. Letting your children write letters to their sponsored 'siblings' will help them appreciate what they have and see those in need as real people, not just generic children starving in Africa.

• Don't discourage their generous acts

If your child wants to give away his favourite toy or asks for charity donations instead of birthday presents, don't say no outright. Make sure he understands the sacrifice he's making, and then let him do it. If he regrets his choice later, encourage him to continue giving to others but suggest some less painful ways to do it.

• When you see your children acting generously, be sure to show your approval

Don't minimise what they do; children may have less to give than adults, but their gifts can make a real difference. Plus, they are forming habits that will continue into adulthood, and their generosity may even encourage you to find more ways to help others!

Here are a few more ideas:

- Have a family conversation about what you're thankful for. This will help your child realise that what they value may be missing in other people's lives.

- Start a tradition in which family members set aside one of their gifts to give to someone less fortunate.

- Think of someone without a family – a soldier, a distant relative, a friend in hospital – and write a letter as a family to make the person feel loved and included during the holidays.

- Talk about beginning the New Year with a family giving box. Everyone can regularly add a small amount of money to the box to contribute to a group or cause the family agrees to support.

Giving offers children a sense of pride and self-esteem. Giving is addictive. It gets in your blood. It makes you realise that you and your actions matter.

Family activity idea 14.1

Setting up a sharing jar or bank

For many families, giving is as important as saving. If that's your philosophy, begin early by explaining that a certain amount of your child's money should be set aside to help people.

Investigate your options Who decides? The whole family can pool its money and give to one or several agreed-upon causes. If so, the family should meet and decide together, weighing the pros and cons of the various organisations. A child might want to give toys to other needy children. In most cases, giving is a very individual thing. A child who has lost a grandparent to a disease may decide to support the search for a cure. If so, help your child find a reputable organisation that supports such research.

Celebrate generosity Recognise the donation as an accomplishment. When the child has enough money saved to make a donation, turn that donation into an event. Carefully count out the money, and then write a cheque to the organisation. You and your child should mail the cheque together and talk about it at the dinner table and with friends.

Send the message Talk about helping others. Whenever you can, make the point that we all help each other. Show it in small ways. For example, ask your child to move an elderly neighbour's newspaper off the lawn onto the porch as he passes the house

194

on the way to school. Work from very local events to more national or international ways in which families help others.

Help your child plan Set your giving goal. How much to give? Children with generous allowances and not many expenses can afford to give more. If the allowance is used to pay many or most of the child's expenses, then she might give less money but her time instead – volunteering.

Illustrate the point Add it up. Help your child understand how a little donation grows. If your child gives 50 cents a week, at the end of six months he or she will have $13 to donate. Count out the coins to make your point.

Decorate the bank Stay focused. Decorate the bank with pictures of a cause that your child wants to give to.

Family activity idea 14.2

Sharing goals worksheet

I'm saving for the next .... months for the following goal(s):

Draw or stick pictures of your goal(s) here

A description of my goal(s):

My goal(s) will cost: $ ....

Lesson 15

Monkey see, monkey do

Your children can learn from your mistakes

Whether we like to admit it or not, we are the products of our parents. Let your children learn from your mistakes instead of repeating them by keeping an open line of communication about money and personal finance. Here are some resources and tools for raising your children with positive money values.

In the course of writing this book, I asked many of my friends how their parents taught them about money. Here is a story I would like to share with you.

John's parents came to this country in the late 50s. Like many others at that time, they had practically no possessions when they arrived and very little money. They had to take odd jobs to scrape by and could barely afford a roof over their heads. Every morning John's dad had to carry two buckets of water up a mountain barefoot in the snow from a well two kilometres away ... okay, John's parents may have exaggerated some of their hardships, but the fact was they didn't have many luxuries.

But they did their best to ensure that John and his siblings had a happy and memorable childhood. They tried their hardest to provide everything children could want and need. In fact, they tried so hard that John grew up a little confused. What could be so confusing about a happy childhood?

He was mainly confused about money. Because his parents never encouraged him to get a job, he never had any money of his own. Whenever he needed cash, he'd have to ask his parents for it. John would ask, and more often than not he would get what he wanted. What was so bad about that?

John had no concept of the value of money. His parents fell into a trap that's all too common. They wanted their children to have a happy childhood, and they probably went without themselves to give him whatever he asked for.

But when you do this, you are also setting your children up for debt or even bankruptcy later on in life. Here are a few of the mistakes parents make around money where their children are concerned.

Using a credit card in front of the children

When you whip out the credit card to pay for your shopping in front of your child, what conclusions are they likely to draw? They see you showing the shop assistant a little plastic card and apparently walking away with a trolley full of shopping for free. Not only do you get to keep the things you bought, you even get your plastic back. You get a whole bunch of stuff for nothing! Looks like a good deal, your child will be thinking!

The child has no idea how much things cost or how many hours it takes to earn the money involved. In John's case, he grew up before credit cards and supermarkets were part of everyday life, but his mother did have a monthly credit account at a department store and he remembers thinking everything she bought there was free. He has fond memories of shopping with his mum, but what was the ultimate consequence?

Now let's fast forward to John in his first year at university. Credit cards were on the scene now, and John had just got his first one. He remembers going nuts at the university bookstore right after activating his card. Then he purchased a year's worth of stationery, assorted clothing and a desk, all in the space of 20 minutes. In fact, John exceeded his credit limit that day (thank goodness for credit limits). It wasn't until his first credit card bill came that John realised how much he'd spent.

But what's this? he asked himself. I only have to pay a few dollars now and I can go on using my card?

Once you get that first bill, it's extremely tempting to pay the minimum balance and continue spending. For many children who have no concept of money, that's exactly how the snowball effect begins.

It's difficult, but parents should try not to model the use of credit cards in front of children. If you do, make sure you let them know how much you've spent and emphasise the value of money in doing so. If John's mum had emphasised the amount of money she was spending on those shopping trips, he might well have had a better concept of value when he got his first credit card.

Buying your children stuff because other kids have it

John grew up in an area of great diversity. Some children came from wealthy families with big houses and expensive cars. Other children were dirt poor, their families couldn't afford cars and they wore secondhand clothes. John's family's circumstances had improved somewhat – they fell somewhere in between.

When John was at high school, he thought there was a strong correlation between the clothes you wore and the car your family drove, and how popular you were with other teenagers. The rich kids really stood out, and most of them were part of the in-crowd.

John wanted to be popular too, but he felt he needed nice stuff in order to fit in. I'm not saying that was wrong in itself, but once he had a credit card he started to feel that he was entitled to luxuries.

Not telling your children how much things cost

During his teenage years John had absolutely no clue how much – or little – money his parents had. He had no idea how much the car repayments cost, how much the mortgage on the house was or what their monthly food budget was.

If he'd known their financial situation (which still wasn't all that healthy), he would have been more responsible, and spent less on entertainment and other frivolous expenses. And he would have whined much less about the stuff that he 'absolutely needed' for school.

I think you have to trust your child with monetary information and allow them to learn from it. Anything that demonstrates the value of money or teaches how it's handled and budgeted can be a valuable learning experience for your child.

Perhaps what is most disturbing is that parents make these mistakes with nothing but the best intentions. We want our children to look back with fond memories of a happy childhood and, in most cases, we think that we are doing the right thing. But there are still more mistakes that parents make when it comes to their children and money.

Spending money on your children without telling your spouse

As a child, John had been a master at playing off his parents against each other. His dad was always stricter with money and the parents would often disagree on the subject. John soon realised that his dad was likely to say no to a request for money. So he'd ask his mum instead, and she had a more sympathetic ear.

'I really need these things for school, but Dad doesn't think it's a worthwhile purchase,' he'd tell her.

'Oh what nonsense! What is it that you need? For something this small, your dad doesn't have to know.'

John's mum was a softie when it came to shopping. She always wanted to see John happy, and sometimes she'd buy things for him without his dad's knowledge. It wasn't as though they were sneaking around behind his father's back, but his mum did buy him a lot of things his dad probably never knew about.

But what message did that send John? For one thing, he learned never to ask his dad for anything. If he wanted something, he went directly to Mum. The second message was that it was okay to spend money without his father knowing. It was almost like John and his mum had a conspiracy going on.

I'm sure you can see why these messages are bad. If anything, John learnt that if his dad didn't know about a purchase, the expense didn't really exist. He also learnt that it was okay to be secretive regarding money. To prevent this happening with your child, you need to form a united front with your partner regarding monetary policy. Children are smart and they'll always take advantage of loopholes in the system.

Giving your children money unintentionally

When John was growing up, he made money by scrounging around the house. His parents would leave a few coins here or drop a banknote there. Sometimes they'd give him ten dollars to buy something and never ask for the change. Sometimes John would ask for more money than he needed to fund a particular activity.

Because John didn't have to earn it, the money he scrounged didn't have a lot of value to him. Often he spent it frivolously on food or entertainment. He says now that parents need to be careful about leaving money lying around. He now recognises the value of making children work for their money by doing chores around the house. If he'd had to mow the lawn or rake the leaves, he would have appreciated the money he had more.

Having absolutely no idea where your children spend their money

As a child, John blew most of his cash on worthless stuff. But a child who truly values money, instead of spending it frivolously, will save it for something she really wants to buy, and her determination to buy the item will be steadfast and unwavering. If you observe your child's spending habits, you can spot and fix many money problems early on. It's especially important for parents to know what their children truly value and want. You can usually get a pretty good idea of how your children are developing just by observing what they spend their money on.

Keeping tabs on where they spend their money will also allow you to spot other problems. Here's a good example. One of my high school friends who'd never had any money suddenly started spending up a storm. He bought a new stereo for his car and treated a group of us to an expensive dinner. Where did he get the cash? Turns out he was breaking into vending machines. As his friends, we urged him to stop. Fortunately, we pressured him to do the right thing before he got into big trouble.

What's odd was that his parents had no idea anything was wrong. If they'd noticed his new stereo or taken an interest in what he was buying, they would have known something was amiss. In retrospect, I think my friend broke into vending machines because he wanted to test his parents to see if they were paying attention.

It's hard enough to teach your children about money in the first place. But if you are sabotaging yourself with mistakes at the same time, it's downright impossible.

Using a calendar, establish a regular schedule for family discussion about finances (e.g. a time when they count their savings and receive interest on them). This is especially helpful to younger children.

Discussion topics should include the differences between cash, cheques and credit cards, and also wise spending, how to avoid the use of credit and the advantages of savings. With teenagers also talk about how to economise at home, and alternatives to spending money.

Develop a sense of limits

When you discuss money with children, you help them develop a sense of limits. You are teaching children that the family as a unit has to make choices about how it can spend money. There's only so much to go around – if you spend it on some things, you won't have it for others.

What's more, you don't have to share everything or go into the finer details with children to teach them to value money. Children have to understand that no matter how well off you are, the family does not have a limitless supply of money. The idea that it needs to be used wisely should be an ongoing message.

Teens and money

CAUTION: Contents unsuitable for parents

Parents: Read this introduction and then turn the book over to your teen. If you take these two clichés – money doesn't grow on trees, and the fruit doesn't fall far from the tree – and shake them up, you have the reason why there is a section in this book called 'Teens and money'.

Your teen is probably asking you for money even as you're reading these words. Or maybe you don't have your own children but you've been known to give money to a niece or a nephew, or a friend's child. Raise your hand if you've never told a child money doesn't grow on trees. And if you don't like the idea of money management or financial planning, chances are that child you're thinking about right now doesn't care for it much either. After all, children learn by example.

Most secondary school students would fail a test on money management. Yet today's teenagers belong to the wealthiest generation ever.

This section is written for teenagers, with tips on how to take action in several areas, from budgeting and first jobs to saving for university or other tertiary studies, using a bank and the importance of saving. Show it to your child (or other teens you think could benefit from some basic money talk) and they'll see that the information is friendly and makes sense. What's more, it doesn't sound like some 50-year-old accountant wrote it.

A good life results from good choices

It won't surprise you to hear that, unlike some adults, your mind is open to ideas and you're not afraid to learn new things. In other words, you've got passion for life.

So if you're planning on putting your dreams out there, why not learn some awesome facts about money (and life!) that can help those dreams come true? Think of them as building blocks you can count on to help you make good choices in life.

Maybe you think you don't have to learn about money until you actually have some. Maybe you think the only fact you need to know about money is that it doesn't grow on trees. Listen up! Money is important. But it's also neither good nor bad. It's how you choose to use it that can be good or bad. Money can make life better by getting rid of worry. You can pay your bills or buy a car or complete a uni education. Or it can make life worse (and pretty boring) if the only thing you care about is making money. Money can't buy time, happiness or passion.

The fact is, a good life doesn't result from money, but from making good choices about money. And it's never too early (or too late) to start making good choices. The choices you make today can change your future. And as long as we're talking choices, thanks for choosing to read on!

Start with a plan to control your life

Okay, so we've established that a good life results from good choices. Here's your first opportunity to make one of those choices. Basically, there are two ways to live life: with a purpose, or without one. You can choose to grab hold of life (like you are by reading this), or you can choose to let life grab hold of you (like those who don't complete high school or college). It all comes down to control. So if you want some control over your life, you need to do some planning.

Set some long-term goals

Take a minute to dream about how you want to grab hold of life. What do you want to accomplish in the next three to five years? Do you want to graduate from high school? Buy a car? Start university? Find a cure for cancer? Go on your OE? Become a millionaire?

Write your long-term goals in the space provided or on another piece of paper. (Don't worry; they're not etched in stone! You can change your mind any time.)

[Space left intentionally blank in original book]

Set some short-term goals

To achieve your long-term goals, you'll also need to set some short-term ones. For example, if you want to get into a top university, you'll need to achieve top grades. So what do you want to accomplish in the next month or so? Ace a stats test? Complete a book report? Lose five kilos? Clean out your wardrobe? Save enough money for a new iPod? Write your short-term goals below:

[Space left intentionally blank in original book]

Now look back over your list. And while you're at it, why not share this list with your parents. How realistic are your goals? For example, you might not be able to lose five kilos in a month, but you can probably lose two. Understate rather than overstate your goals so you don't get disappointed. And remember, it's always easier to reach your goals when you take them one step at a time.

Keep a 'to do' list

In a business, employees aren't expected to remember all the specific things they have to do at specific times. No, they write all that stuff down. So can you. A 'to do' list helps you remember everything you need to do each day toward reaching your goals. Think of it as a way to declutter your mind. Instead of carrying around reminders on Post-it notes or napkins, keep your own daily 'to do' list and calendar.

Here are some tips:

- Figure out your peak time of day. Attack difficult things when you are sharpest mentally.

- Build your day around important stuff; schedule less important stuff for the time left over.

- Set deadlines. Make them specific.

- Don't over-schedule. Be aware of your time limitations.

- Allow a time cushion. Don't cram every minute with activities. Provide for the unexpected.

- Get help if you need it. Sometimes you can't do it alone, and that's okay.

- Don't forget to schedule your chores.

- Reward yourself when you reach a goal.

- Take time to daydream. Or to do absolutely nothing at all!

Remember: When you take care of the minutes, the hours take care of themselves.

Making money

Before you spend money, you have to earn it.

Like I said earlier, money can make life better by getting rid of worry. You can pay your bills or buy a car or complete a uni education. But sometimes it's cool just to have money for stuff like music, movies and new clothes. Maybe you already have some extra cash stashed away from your allowance or a birthday or holiday gift from your grandparents. Maybe you'd like a lot more cash. If so, you'll need to earn it by getting a job.

Think about your skills and interests

Write down what you like to do and what you think you do well. Do you like the outdoors? If so, you might consider mowing lawns or gardening or being a lifeguard at a local pool. Do you like being around lots of people? How about working in a restaurant or music store? If you are having trouble figuring out what you'd like to do:

- Go to your school guidance counsellor and ask to take an Interest Inventory.

- Talk to friends and relatives. What skills do they think you have? What kind of work do they suggest for you?

- Check out the library. Your school or local library is loaded with information about jobs: what they demand and what training you need. Many also have easy-to-use websites that match skills with jobs.

Figure out how much time you can spend working

Here are a couple of suggestions to help you:

- Talk to your parents. You may need their help with your job, especially if you need to arrange transport. How much time can they give?

- Set up a schedule. How much time do you need to set aside for chores, schoolwork and extracurricular activities? Are you prepared to give up nights out with friends or your favourite TV show?

Find out what jobs are out there

There are probably more ways than you realise to go about this. You can:

- Talk to your friends, relatives, neighbours, teachers and counsellors. Word of mouth is always the best way to find a job.

- Notice the notices! Check out 'help wanted' signs in windows, newspaper ads, bulletin boards at libraries, community centres and local businesses.

- Surf the internet.

- Think about working for yourself. Maybe you have a great idea for making money on your own. Plus there are tons of books that offer great ideas.

Ace the application and interview

The most important thing to remember about a job application and interview is that first impressions mean everything (even though first impressions can sometimes be wrong). When you go to your interview, which often entails filling out an application, dress conservatively. That doesn't necessarily mean you show up looking like a Member of Parliament or a banker, but don't show up dressed like Pink, Snoop Dogg or Marilyn Manson. And remember to:

- Tell the truth. Employers will check everything you write down or say.

- Bring your own pen.

- Know your Inland Revenue or tax file number.

- Find out as much as you can about the company or business.

- Make a list of questions like: 'What are my duties?' 'When can I start work?' 'What benefits do you offer?' Ask at least one specific question about what the store or company does. It shows you did your homework.

- Practise the interview with a friend or relative. The employer might ask: 'Why should I hire you?' and, 'What are your strengths?'

- Be polite. Say 'Thank you' (after 'I'm sorry', the two most important words in the English language).

Here's one last thing to think about for the long term: sometimes the job that makes you the happiest (and sometimes also the most money) is one where what you most want to do meets up with what the world most needs you to do. Like being a cancer research scientist. Or a social justice activist. Maybe even a poet. In other words, a job where you become the best you can be by helping the world become the best it can be.

Needs and wants

Spend money on needs before wants.

Every year, teens around the world spend billions of dollars on stuff. For that reason, huge clothing, music and soft drink companies spend millions on advertising to suck you into buying the latest, the greatest, the coolest sport shoes, jeans or MP3 players. Besides, your best friend is wearing cool new shoes and you want them too. Plus, you've got the cash. You don't have to pay for rent, electricity or the groceries. So why not just go ahead and spend your money on whatever you want?

Well, for one thing, it's not how the real world works. Before you know it you'll be out of school and responsible for paying your own bills. Even before that time, you'll need to save money for a tertiary education or a car. Now is the time to discipline yourself to buy what you need before you buy what you want. Here are four easy suggestions on how to start.

Keep a spending diary

Get a small notebook. Carry it with you in your pocket, backpack or purse. Write down every purchase you make for a week. Drinks, video games, shoes, birthday cards, lunch, a movie – everything. At the end of the week, take a close look at your purchases. Total up the things you had to buy. Now total up everything else. What are your spending habits? How much can you save if you cut out a couple of soft drinks every week? Or one takeaway lunch?

Maintain a budget

Stop rolling your eyes! Maintaining a monthly budget makes a lot of sense (not to mention cents). A budget works for companies and governments, and it can work for you.

- Figure out your monthly income. Add up the money you get for an allowance plus any money you earn regularly at a part-time job. If your income varies from month to month (for example, you might baby-sit more often around the holidays), figure out an average amount.

- Figure out your monthly expenses. Total up the things you have to buy each month. Do you have to buy your own school lunches? Take a bus to piano lessons? Or a part-time job?

• Add up what you have left over. That's what you can spend (and save!) every month.

Evaluate all those ads

You don't believe everything adults tell you, so don't believe everything magazine ads or TV commercials tell you. There is no product that will make you more beautiful or smarter or cooler. Only you can do that (and, face it, you're pretty cool already).

And keep in mind that you pay for advertising. That's right – about 20% to 40% of what you paid for those sneakers went to that top sports star who's paid millions to wear them. So the next time you're caught up in the emotion of an ad, step back and be realistic. You're only getting the good news about that brand. Not the bad news – like its outrageous price!

Comparison shop

Once you've got some well-earned cash for something like a new MP3 player, don't drop it all on the first player you listen to.

• Do some research. Check out consumer reports at the library or consumer websites. They rate all sorts of products, based on a range of tests.

- Talk to an expert. Talk to your parents and friends who own an MP3 player. What do they like, or not, about it?

- Compare prices in newspaper ads, or on PriceSpy. Look for sales. What are the hidden costs?

- Think twice before spending money on an extended warranty.

- Check out the classifieds or an online auction. You might be surprised at how affordable a used, but solid, product can be. Don't overlook garage sales, either.

Some keys to owning a car

Your first set of wheels is a big deal – in more ways than one. A car (even a used one) costs big bucks to buy and more big bucks to drive. The average cost of driving a 1990 car for 10,000 kilometres a year for four years is around $2500 a year.

And don't forget about car insurance. (If you're in Australia, third party insurance is compulsory.) Car insurance protects you against money losses connected to your car. It helps you pay for medical care and car repairs if you and others are in an accident. Car insurance is not cheap, especially if you're a guy under 25. You can save money on insurance by taking a defensive driving course, getting good grades and maintaining a safe driving record.

Credit cards

It's not free money

Oh, how credit card companies love teens! How much do they love you? So much that by the time you're 18 (the age when a credit card company can legally force you to pay them back), they'll have convinced you to sign up for more than one credit card.

Here's what credit card companies *don't* tell you:

- Most credit card accounts are compound interest loans in disguise. When you buy something with your card and don't pay it back within 45 days or so, the credit card company treats it as a loan, often at very high interest – between 18% and 20%. Think of it as owing them 20 cents for every dollar they 'lend' you. And it gets worse.

- Instead of forcing you to pay off this 'loan' in a certain amount of time, the credit card company says, 'No problemo. You only have to make minimum payments each month.' Then they suggest a small amount. It's pretty tempting to pay only that small amount, isn't it? Keep reading.

- The interest you owe for that month may be more than the minimum payment. So what does this credit card company do with that unpaid interest? It adds it to your balance. Next month, you're not only paying interest on what you borrowed, you're

220

paying interest on interest. Good grief, this can't get much worse. Or can it?

- Whoops, the credit card company that loves you so much hasn't said anything about paying back the principal, or the original amount you paid for that spring wardrobe and MP3 player. You're making payments, but the balance is going up. Hold on a second, this next part can't possibly be true, can it?

- If you're late with your payment, or go over your credit limit, you're charged a fee which that nice credit card company adds to your balance. Now you're paying interest on everything.

On top of that, not paying off your credit cards can give you a poor credit rating. Credit rating agencies keep track of debts you don't pay on time. Stores, banks and other financial institutions have access to these files. A poor credit rating can keep you from getting more credit in the future. It's like a black mark on your record. You may not be able to get a loan to buy a car or a home for a number of years.

Yes, there'll be times when it will be great to have a credit card to get something you really need (and you don't have enough cash), or to get yourself out of a jam. But more often than not a credit card will get you into a jam. Don't be fooled.

Curb the impulsive spending

There's a reason why chocolate bars are so conveniently located at supermarket or convenience store check-out lanes. So many consumers suffer from a 'must-have' mentality that eats away their money. You see a great looking shirt and you MUST HAVE IT NOW! Stop!

Take only enough money with you each day to cover your needs. When you shop, take a list of things you need and stick to it. Walk away from the item you want to buy and think about it. Ninety per cent of the time, you won't return.

Pay your bills on time

Do this and you won't have to worry about interest payments, and you won't get trapped into paying off one credit card with another one. And stay within your credit limit. If you go over your limit, you'll pay a penalty and possibly have your card privileges suspended.

Choose a credit card that won't rip you off

- Look for a card with a low interest rate. Beware of 'teaser' rates though. Some companies only charge a small percentage, but after six months it jumps to 18% or more!

- Compare the yearly charges. Most store cards don't have yearly fees.

- Check for any special fees or penalty payments. You don't want to pay extra charges (on top of interest) for being late or for not using your card.

- Choose a card that charges you interest on your 'balance due', not on your 'average daily balance'. The second will cost you more money.

- Choose a card that has a 'grace period'. This means that you are not charged interest on your balance until after the payment due date. Some cards charge interest from the time of purchase. This too will cost you more money.

- Some cards earn you money. They give you back 1–3% of your yearly credit total if you pay your balance in full each month.

- Don't let offers of free T-shirts, trips or discounts confuse you. Don't let anyone hurry you into making a decision. Read the fine print!

Saving money

It's your money, so pay yourself first

Most people pay everyone else first, and then themselves. This is screwed up. It's your money. So why not pay yourself first? It's called savings. The numbers show that you do just the opposite: every year, teens earn millions of dollars from summer and part-time jobs and spend almost all of it.

But you're smart. You don't want to spend 100% of what you earn. You've decided that you want to sock away at least 10% into savings for uni, a car or an emergency (like if your car breaks down). Good for you. The earlier you start the habit of saving, the better.

There's this amazing thing called interest

If you keep your money in a wallet or your dresser drawer, it's safe – but that's about it. Put in five dollars and take out five dollars. But when you open a savings account at a bank, your money starts to appreciate (grow) thanks to interest. Interest is a percentage of the balance in your account that the bank pays you to use your money to make loans to other customers. When it lends your money to someone else, it charges that customer interest at a higher percentage than the rate paid to you. For example, a bank might pay you 2% to 4% interest on your savings and offer loans at 8% to 10% interest, or lower depending on the economic climate.

Simple interest is when a bank pays you a certain percentage of every dollar you save. If you've got $1000 in the bank (your principal) and the bank pays you 3% annual interest, you get three cents on each dollar every year. At the end of the year, you will have earned $30 on your $1000.

There's an even more amazing thing called compounding

Most banks pay compound interest. This means that you earn interest not just on the dollars you put into your savings, but also on the interest itself. So what's the big deal? Try this out: the next time you want to ask your parents for 20 bucks, ask them instead for five cents that doubles in value every day for a month. As this chart shows you, by the end of the month, they'll owe you $26.8 million.

The power of doubling five cents a day

Day	Amount
1	$0.05
2	$0.10
3	$0.20
4	$0.40
5	$0.80
6	$1.60
7	$3.20
8	$6.40
9	$12.80
10	$25.60
11	$51.20
12	$102.40
13	$204.80

Day	Amount
14	$409.60
15	$819.20
16	$1,638.40
17	$3,276.80
18	$6,553.60
19	$13,107.20
20	$26,214.40
21	$52,428.80
22	$104,857.60
23	$209,715.20
24	$419,430.40
25	$838,860.80
26	$1,677,721.60
27	$3,355,443.20
28	$6,710,886.40
29	$13,421,772.80
30	$26,843,545.60

Pretty amazing, right? Okay, okay, we know your parents will never fork out this kind of cash. But you might want to remember a couple of cool rules.

The rule of seven

If you save money for seven years and then stop, you'll accumulate around as much as a person who delays saving during the same seven years, but then starts and continues saving for 45 years! Check this out:

You		The other person	
Save $50 per month from birth to age seven, then stop (seven years)		Saves $50 per month from age seven to 52 (45 years)	
At age 18, the value is:	$22,955	At age 18, the value is:	$13,730
At age 45:	$488,508	At age 45:	$455,837
At age 52:	$1,082,145	At age 52:	$1,083,462

Both cases are based on 12% annual compounded rate of return. You only had to save $4,200. The other person had to save $27,000 to catch up.

The rule of 72
Take the rate of return (the interest rate) on an investment and divide that number into 72. That tells you roughly how long it will take for your investment to double in value. For example, an investment earning 10% annually will double in 7.2 years (72 divided by 10).

Banking

Check out a cheque account

Okay, you've learned some cool stuff about making, spending and, most important, saving money. And you've learned that a good place to save money is in a savings account at a bank that pays compound interest.

One of the most important benefits of a bank is a cheque account. Instead of carrying around a stack of bills or running up a credit card, you can simply and safely write out a cheque. A cheque is like a promise that the bank will pay the amount of the cheque to the business or person who receives it from you.

Most banks require that a person opening a cheque account be 18 and have a full-time job. You may be able to open a cheque account with a parent or guardian, but every time you write a cheque, the adult must co-sign it. (How fun is that?) But don't skip this next part! It's never too early to learn some banking basics.

How a cheque account works:

- money goes into your account when you make a deposit
- money comes out of your account when you write a cheque.

Here's the step-by-step:

1. You deposit money into your cheque account.

2. You use cheques to pay bills or buy something. Your signed cheque is like money.

3. The business or person that receives your cheque deposits it in their bank account and then your bank subtracts it from your account.

4. Your bank takes the money out of your account and gives it to the business or person.

5. You make a note in what is called your cheque register every time you put money in or take money out of your account. Otherwise you might lose track of how much money you actually have.

It's a big mistake not to keep track of what's going in and coming out of your account. If there's not enough money in your account to pay for the cheques you write, your cheque 'bounces'. It's also called being 'overdrawn'. The bank sends you a notice in the mail and charges you a hefty fee. Don't write a cheque if your account can't cover it.

How to make deposits:

• Take the money to the bank.

• Mail the money to the bank (cheques only).

• Put the money directly into an ATM (automated teller machine). Remember, ATMs do not print money! Using an ATM – or debit – card with a personalised identification number (PIN), you have instant access to your cheque or savings account. When you get money from the machine, you're actually taking money out of your account. If your account is empty, the machine won't cough up any money.

Here's the step-by-step procedure:

1. Complete a deposit slip (they're behind the cheques in your cheque book).

2. Write the deposit in your cheque register.

How to write cheques

Look at the cheque sample on this page. In order for a cheque to be valid, all the blanks must be completed.

Note that the amount of the cheque must be written in both numbers and words. For example, if the cheque is for $34.12, you must write 'Thirty-four dollars and 12 cents'. This may not make sense to you, but writing the dollar amount both ways protects you. For example, if your cheque is for $100, some loser might be tempted to add a zero to the $100 and cash your cheque for $1000. When you write out the number in words, it's pretty hard to make 'one hundred' look like 'one thousand'.

Keeping your account balanced
Now that you know how a cheque account works, you might be tempted to actually open one with a bank near you. If you do, don't forget how important it is to keep an accurate record of how much money you put into the account, and how much you take out.

Money works

Before you invest, investigate

More than ever before, teenagers like you are taking a step beyond saving money in accounts that offer simple interest. They are investing money, especially in the share market.

The share market is always in the news, so it makes sense that you're curious about making money that way. Plus, the government superannuation may not be around when you'll need it for retirement in about 50 years. Investing money (like that tidy sum you inherited from your grandmother) in shares may be a smart way to grow your money over the long term. But remember, the higher the rate of return you expect on an investment, the higher the risk. Before you invest, always investigate.

Stocks are shares in a company. When you invest in a company's stock or buy its shares, you own part of the company. You become a stockholder (or shareholder). Here are the pros of investing in stocks:

- Historically, shares have outperformed other investments, such as bank accounts, bonds, fixed interest, property, etc. You may earn a 10% to 12% average annual rate of return in shares over a decade or more, but put on a seat belt because, year-to-year, it can be a wild rollercoaster ride! Average annual returns may go way up or way down over time.

- As a shareholder you have voting rights when the company wants to make particular changes. You don't at a bank.

Here are the cons:

- Share prices aren't guaranteed. They go up and down, so don't forget the seat belt.

- You can lose some, or all, of your money.

To decide on a stock to buy, look for:

- A company that interests you or produces something you think is cool like clothes, music or computer games.

- A company that makes money and has potential to grow. Contact the company (get the address from its website or the library) for its annual report, which will tell you how much money the company made last year and in previous years. You can view these reports at the company's website too.

- After you decide on a stock you want to buy, you'll need a parent to set up an account with an adult named as a custodian to approve any transactions. Keep in mind, too, that buying and selling stocks does cost money. You have to pay a broker to do the actual buying and selling for you.

What do those funny words mean?

One of the smartest things you can do is to keep track of your investment by reading the stock tables. These are those columns of tiny numbers found in the financial pages of your newspaper. Here's how (and once you get the hang of it, explain it to your parents!).

Sample newspaper per share price table

Company name	Last sale price	"+ or -"	Quote Buyer	Seller	52 Week High	Low	Dividend Rate	Yield %	PE Ratio
AGL Energy Ltd	14.5	+49	14.48	14.56	16.47	10.20	53.00	3.66	27.6
AMP Ltd	6.5	+15	6.48	6.51	10.97	6.01	46.00p	7.08	12.2
ANZ Banking Grp	15.91	+24	15.90	15.93	31.74	15.32	136.00f	8.55	7.5
ASX Ltd	35.10	+99	36.07	36.13	61.00	28.28	192.40f	5.48	16.4
BHP Billiton	40.00	-15	39.97	40.00	50.00	31.00	78.83f	1.97	14.0
Coca-Cola Amatil	8.13	-15	8.12	8.15	10.75	6.65	37.00f	4.55	17.7
CSL Ltd	36.89	+102	38.69	38.70	43.19	30.90	46.00f	1.19	30.3

See Bid* See Offer* See Div* See PE*

Price range for 52 weeks See Yld%*

Hi Lo The highest and lowest prices for each stock are shown for the last 52 weeks. These figures demonstrate the stock's volatility, or the stock's upside profit potential and downside risk.

Stock Stocks are listed by company names that are abbreviated and listed alphabetically. Each company has a ticker symbol that resembles the name of the company or is related to what the company does.

Bid The price an investor is willing to pay for a security.

Security A document or other means that proves the ownership of stocks, bonds and other investments by investors.

Offer The lowest price an investor will accept to sell a stock.

Div Every quarter, many companies pay shareholders a dividend, a portion of the company's profits for each share they own. If this column is blank, that means the company doesn't pay cash dividends.

Yld % The per cent yield is how much dividend you get for the amount you pay. This column is blank when there is no dividend.

PE The price earning ratios (PE ratio) is the relationship between the price of one share of stock and the annual earnings per share of the company. For example, if a company has a PE ratio of 25, that means you could buy one share of stock for 25 times what the company earned per share during the past year.

Vol 100s This figure, times 100, is the volume of shares traded on the previous day.

Hi Lo Close These columns show the highest, lowest and closing price of the stock on the previous day.

Net Chg The net change compares the closing price of your stock on this day with the closing price from the previous day. A minus sign means the closing price on this day is lower than the previous day. A plus sign means it's higher. Stocks that showed a price change of 5% or more are listed in a bold font.

Tertiary education costs money

To university or to work? That is the question. Maybe Shakespeare never had to make that call, but you will. Perhaps you'll decide to work for a couple of years, and then get more education. Or perhaps you'll want to get more education right away. Whatever you decide, remember you'll always benefit from more education, and it's never too late to learn more.

You probably know that the more educated you are, the more money you can make in your lifetime. The average New Zealand and Australian university graduate (BA degree) earned $49,674 a year in 2004, compared to just $26,059 a year for non-graduates. That's a 90% earnings advantage, up from 57% in 1975. By the time you've got your diploma, the numbers may be even better!

You can earn a bachelor's degree from a three-year university course in all areas of study from history, languages, music and art to computer science, nursing, engineering and business. If you're really ambitious, think about completing a master's degree or a doctorate.

What about polytechnics and technical colleges? These schools offer diplomas and certificates qualifying you for work in diverse fields. Among the jobs you can qualify for: mechanic, cosmetologist, graphic artist, electrician, practical nurse, computer technician or childcare professional. Some institutes have programmes devoted to just one area, such as business or the arts.

Paying for your education

Save your money before you go to university or a tertiary institute (see Lesson 3 on the difference between needs and wants). There are also a variety of other funding options available if you're motivated to look for them:

- Receive a grant from a university or the government. These are great because you don't have to pay them back. The amount is simply subtracted from your tuition bill.

- Apply for scholarships from universities or organisations. Many universities, businesses, community organisations and foundations award scholarships for good grades, good extracurricular activities or good citizenship. But you have to apply! Go to the library or surf the internet for scholarship databases that match your personal and educational profile with scholarship money.

- Get student loans from the government or from a bank. You borrow money when you get a loan. What's more, you agree to pay it back with interest. Some government loans in New Zealand, however, are interest-free on certain conditions.

- Thankfully, there are a number of loan programmes offered by Australian banks and state governments that can help you get the money you need to support yourself while you study. Many of these offer deferred payments until after you complete your studies, and some also offer deferred interest. You need to evaluate all your loan options carefully to choose the right student loan for your needs.

You can save a bundle of money by challenging certain assumptions about university and finding more frugal alternatives. Like living at home. Eating only once or twice a week. Hey, if you cut out food altogether, going to university won't seem so important any more ... Think of the money you'd save!

When thinking about university or other tertiary institutions, don't overlook the fact that you'll make more money in your lifetime by going, but you'll also benefit in many more ways. You'll make lifelong friends, and maybe meet your future mate. Most of all, you'll make amazing discoveries about the past, the future and the present ... the earth, the sun and the Milky Way ... Shakespeare and Plato ... bytes, megabytes and gigabytes ... algorithms, numerators and transcendental functions. And the list goes on, but we don't want to take up too much of your time.

A word to parents

CAUTION: Contents unsuitable for teens

Teens, turn the book back over to your parents now – they need to know a few things about your education.

University funding

A little knowledge can go a long, long way

We always tell it like it is. So here's the bad news about paying for your children's university expenses. No matter how old your children are today, it's going to cost a whole lot of money to send them to university. For a bachelor's degree in Australia, annual tuition fees range from AU$3847 to AU$8018. In New Zealand, according to the New Zealand University Students Association (NZUSA), fees range from NZ$4217 to NZ$5644. Living expenses are additional.

When you factor in inflation, the number of years it will be until your child heads off to university and the budgetary whims of governments, and then multiply that figure by the three or four years it will take to earn a degree, let's just say we're hoping your calculator can handle the result.

But there is good news! The average New Zealand and Australian university graduate (BA degree) earned $49,674 a year in 2004, compared to just $26,059 a year for non-graduates. That's a 90% earnings advantage, up from 57% in 1975. Those figures aren't for entry-level jobs of course. But they paint a rosy picture of the earnings potential of university grads in general.

Of course, attending university isn't just about making lots of money. It's about attending lots of parties and other events and setting world records for how many people you can jam into a new Mini. Stuff like that. Clearly, a university education has a potential value going way beyond opportunities for bonding with fellow students in a compact car. It's an investment that may pay dividends for a lifetime – pardon the financial cliché, but it sure holds true in this case.

Anyway, here's a little knowledge that can go a long way toward helping you overcome your fear, loathing, confusion and Stage I panic on the subject of paying for tertiary education.

Things you should know about tertiary education funding

Here are some talking points on the subject:

1. When it comes to financing university, it's never too early to start. It's never too late either, so don't give up before you've begun.

2. Take heart from the fact that despite all the soaring costs and scary calculations, paying for your children's university education is quite likely going to be a mix of things that are both available and feasible.

3. There are literally dozens of vehicles to help you save and invest for education. It's going to take some homework to wade through them and decide what's best for you, but it's a good way to invest your time.

4. Check with a financial adviser about options.

5. Don't count on scholarships. Don't discount scholarships, either. With some diligence, you may actually find some are available to your children.

6. Taking out a home equity loan for university financing may get your children an education, but it could prove to be a hard lesson on bad financial planning for you.

Don't delay planning and saving
It's better to start financing university early for a lot of obvious reasons. In the end, though, paying for your children's university is quite likely going to be a mix of savings, some type of financial aid, loans, possibly some paid work on the part of the student (it's good for them), and even gifts from grandparents or other relatives. Just don't count on lottery winnings.

Newborn to ten years

Consider investments that have the potential to grow in value, like shares or managed funds. You may want to look for managed funds that primarily buy shares in companies that are poised to expand and grow in the future. Each fund has specific investment goals, and a common objective is growth. Growth funds are designed to produce capital gains rather than a flow of dividends. Investors who buy growth funds are more interested in seeing the fund's unit price rise faster than the mercury on the Gold Coast than in receiving income from dividends. Many managed funds will accept small monthly investments, and there's a tremendous variety to choose from.

However, growth funds carry more risk and can be more volatile than investments with a fixed income. With that risk and volatility generally comes the potential for a greater return, which may eliminate having to crawl on your knees to Aunt Gertrude.

Ten to 14 years

You have between four and eight years to invest. Don't panic (although Grandpa is looming a bit larger in the picture). Consider a balanced investment portfolio consisting of growth funds, plus fixed interest funds, which provide income (be sure to look for the words 'growth' and 'income' in the prospectus).

Typically, longer-term bonds provide higher interest rates. A fixed interest fund invests in corporate or government bonds. All fixed interest funds are subject to interest rate risk, and most are subject to credit risk. A balanced portfolio combines investments in preferred shares, common shares and bonds.

Balanced managed funds generally have three objectives:

1. Get the children out of the house.

2. Teach them how to do their own laundry.

3. Show them how much you love them.

Actually, the three objectives of balanced managed funds are to conserve initial principal, pay current income and promote long-term growth of principal and income.

Over 14

Do you live near a casino? Just kidding. Consider investments for income and liquidity, such as income-oriented managed funds (look for the word 'income' in the prospectus and remember, don't do this late at night unless you need something to help you sleep). Also consider limited maturity bonds and fixed interest funds. These are intended to provide moderate growth without sacrificing stability and liquidity. You can move into either fixed-income securities, money market instruments (highly liquid funds that pay current interest rates), or other savings vehicles timed to mature when tuition is due.

Talking to teens about your finances/the financial crisis

What younger children need most is reassurance. Older children can process more information both at school and at home, though getting the details straight sometimes presents challenges of its own.

Taking advantage of this teachable moment doesn't have to be limited to the economics class. Teachers could inject financial literacy into social studies by explaining how borrowers overextended themselves on mortgages and credit-card debt. And in maths class, students could use a compounding calculator to learn how it would pay for young people to buy shares at today's fire-sale prices.

At home, too, parents can use various strategies to reassure teenagers while giving them a lesson in managing money.

Being proactive

You don't have to share every detail of your family's finances. But if you need to reduce your spending because of a layoff or because you want to pay off debt, show your children how your monthly expenses stack up with your income and how you plan to cut back. That puts your finances in context without overloading the children with information.

Having a plan teens can participate in

Perhaps they can cover some of their own expenses by taking on more baby-sitting gigs or mowing more lawns.

If paying tuition fees is an issue, have an up-front discussion about what you can afford. Should they attend a university locally rather than attend a university that involves accommodation costs? Does it make sense to borrow based on their potential future income?

And if your children are already studying and you're suddenly short of cash, you have options. Your children may be eligible for a student allowance.

Being positive and adding perspective

From time to time serious economic downturns occur. Teens and young adults may never have experienced a recession before. They need to know that our economies have always recovered from such crises in the past, and that the same is likely to be true of any they experience in the future.

Your child's flying start

Australia

Schools get 'A' for effort

We are all aware of the financial effects of poor money management skills. These effects have impacted on many of us since the 2008 crash. But good money management skills start at school, and should become an essential part of learning in the 21st century.

Australian schoolchildren are now being taught skills in money management as part of a framework that has been put together by a federal agency, the Ministerial Council on Education, Employment, Training and Youth Affairs (MCEETYA), with the aim of increasing financial literacy in Australia. In bureaucratic terms, the aim is to 'relate personal financial education to existing curriculum' and 'provide young people with opportunities to identify, engage with and discuss "real world" financial contexts'. In other words, this programme is not only for schools, but is also targeting adults and children through a range of initiatives.

In Lesson 1 ('The sooner you start, the less scary it will be') we looked at the different stages of financial development, and it seems this framework has taken these concepts onboard. While at school, your child's progress is followed closely by teachers looking at what they should be achieving at different stages of their education, starting at Year 3. Year 3 involves children understanding, for example, the concept of money – not just coins and notes, but cheques and debit or credit cards, where money comes from and the need for families to budget, the difference between wants and needs, and how money can be saved.

These stages are outlined in two-year increments, so that by Year 5 children are taught a beginner's guide to their rights and responsibilities in connection with making money and financial transactions, as well as an awareness of peer pressure and the social environment. By Year 9 they should be able to keep simple personal financial records, determine financial goals and assess investment risk and return from basic information.

The way this programme is taught varies from school to school. One approach has been the creation of the Financial Literacy Foundation, a not-for-profit organisation that aims to improve financial literacy across the Australian population as a whole. The foundation has been given an initial total budget of $5 million a year indexed until 2008/9 and reviewed annually, as well as $16 million for an information programme. Among its activities is the provision of literacy programmes, working with schools and teachers to provide the lessons.

There are also a number of programmes with support materials and resources sponsored by commercial organisations. For example, the National Savings Challenge (NSC) fits within the requirements of the MCEETYA framework and has been put together for primary schools by an independent business called Kids Money. Kids Money has created a kit that includes a ready-to-use ten-week lesson plan. The school has to register to take part in the challenge, but once registered the teaching resources, such as the lesson plan and the NSC supplies, are provided free of charge.

Sorry parents, but you don't get off scot-free. These lesson plans include homework parents need to be involved in, such as helping your children to earn money and helping them to allocate it to key areas. As the programme is a challenge there are awards made quarterly. The prizes are educational and are judged not on the amount earned but on the creativity shown in earning and saving.

Another recent addition to the support for education in schools is the BIG WIN Financial Literacy Program. This is aimed at middle- and upper-level primary school children between the ages of seven and 12, and is provided by enRICH KIDS. This programme has also been endorsed by the Financial Literacy Foundation and provides teaching plans, worksheets and suggested activities as well as certificates of achievement for teachers to use. As this is a paid programme, your child's activity fees may go up by another $34.95, but the investment is worth it. Other books and support materials are also available for parents to purchase.

We all know that our children are cent$ational, but just so that we don't forget, the Bank of Queensland is sponsoring an undertaking by the *Ethical Investor* magazine with the development of a school play aimed at primary and junior school children, teaching them about money. The play has the catchy title *Cent$ational Harry* and teaches the money concepts outlined in the MCEETYA framework. The character Harry is a school dropout who's failing financially. He's visited by aliens, and learns by teaching the aliens about money and making financial mistakes. The play is put on at a charge of $6 per student, or $10 per family (plus GST).

Don't worry – your older children don't miss out either. The Commonwealth Bank of Australia may be seen as the major supporter of education in schools, with a number of approaches aimed at children. The Commonwealth Bank Foundation was created in 2003 with the aim of encouraging financial education through capturing the minds of young Australians. The bank offers 100 Commonwealth Bank Foundation Literacy Grants of $3500 each year (applications open in May and close in August) to Australian schools. The grants are provided so that schools can invest further in financial education.

Commonwealth Bank staff also make an appearance in the classroom through the StartSmart Schools programme aimed at secondary schools. Information is delivered not by teachers, but by trained bank staff. Your children will be exposed to a set of different modules from which the school can choose some or all. These include modules on bank accounts, earning an income, and managing money and investing. The bank provides the resources needed and encourages the students to start earning and saving. Each workshop offered lasts two hours. So don't be offended if you receive the odd promotional flyer in your child's backpack.

The bank also provides teachers and schools with free access to the website www.dollarsandsense.com.au.

This gives your child's teacher a vast range of teaching resources that can be used with students between 14 and 18. The website is also student-friendly, with appropriate information available for your child to access at any time.

But wait, there's more – your child's very own financial gymboree. The Commonwealth Bank holds StartSmart financial literacy forums; some are aimed at the 16–24 age group, and there are also forums aimed at teachers to support their personal development skills and confidence in teaching financial literacy. To ensure your child is on track, the Australian Financial Literacy Assessment is a tool developed by the Commonwealth Bank. This tool is designed to enable schools to look at students in Years 9 and 10 in order to assess their level of financial literacy.

Remember, though, that however strong and well-established this programme is, it's provided by a bank, and while it's run through the bank's charitable foundation, there is still a strong probability of commercial motivation behind the project in support of the uptake of student bank accounts.

However, primary and high school children need to be taught essential life skills to help them survive and thrive in our society. Money management skills are an essential part of a modern education and any efforts that governments and private organisations make as part of this crusade are to be applauded – the pros outweigh the cons.

Yes, it could be all about politics or money. But in the past our children weren't taught money management in schools because there were limited budgets and no support for it. Those days have past, and Australia is taking a positive stance in its attempt to address the financial illiteracy of earlier generations.

Your child's flying start

New Zealand

KiwiSaver for kids

A sage once said that it takes more than money to make men rich. But the practically-minded among us also know that a little money can be very useful – most of all because it affords us choice in what we do. With this in mind it makes excellent sense to put some money aside regularly and watch it grow into a nest egg for your child. And, as they say, the earlier you start saving the better, not only from a financial security perspective but also because you'll acquire the actual discipline of saving.

As the American statesman and philosopher Benjamin Franklin (1706–1790) said, 'Money makes money, and the money money makes, makes more money.'

Having some financial security by the time your child reaches adulthood means that there are many more choices open to her. Look at things from a child's perspective. Perhaps she wants to study at university? Maybe she just wants her own car or to do the 'big OE'? These things cost money, so it pays to start planning well in advance. The right savings plan, along with your encouragement and a guiding hand, will help ensure your child realises her dreams and aspirations.

There are various vehicles available to save for your children's education and future. One of these is KiwiSaver.

With no minimum age to join, the government incentives attached to KiwiSaver make it a great way to put aside money for your children's future (see Lesson 9, 'Laughing all the way to the bank').

Starting early, compound interest and regular savings can do more than you think. The table shows how an account balance could grow with various contribution amounts.

Years	No contributions	$20 per month	$40 per month
starting balance	$1,000	$1,000	$1,000
1	$1,060	$1,280	$1,501
5	$1,338	$2,728	$4,118
10	$1,791	$5,040	$8,290
15	$2,397	$8,135	$13,873
20	$3,207	$12,276	$21,345

Assumes savings earn 6% per year net of fees and taxes, and 3% inflation.

What happens if they take on a job?

As a KiwiSaver member, unless your child is on a contribution holiday they'll have to notify their employer to deduct KiwiSaver contributions from their wages, at a minimum rate of 2%. Under the current rules it's possible to apply for a contribution holiday after being a KiwiSaver member for 12 months.

What contributions are required?

For those not receiving a salary or wages there is no minimum ongoing contribution level to KiwiSaver, although you'll need to make an initial contribution to open the account. After that you can choose the contribution amounts and how frequently they are made.

How are contributions made?

Contributions can be made in a number of ways:

- using the 'pay tax' option on your internet banking facility

- making a payment over the counter at a bank branch or directly to Inland Revenue

- direct to a scheme provider via online banking or other means.

All of these methods allow relatives (such as parents or grandparents) to make a KiwiSaver contribution on behalf of the account holder.

Finding money when you don't have any

If you don't have money left over, then you are in good company – most New Zealanders don't. How can you save for tertiary education or your child's KiwiSaver when you don't have any extra cash? Start by analysing your spending habits.

Take a good look at your budget (if you require assistance, check out my previous book, *Budget Wise, Dollar Rich).* Is there any thing in your budget you can eliminate? Are there any costs you can reduce?

Did you know that if you reduce spending by just $2 a day and put that into savings, you could put aside almost $6000 in five years? So really challenge yourself. Maybe you'll find more than a couple of dollars. Here are some suggested ways to save a dollar (or three):

- cut out your morning coffee

- clip coupons and review flyers to reduce the cost of groceries

- turn down your heating by 2° to save on power

- wash your clothes in cold water

- bring your lunch to work

- check sale items first when buying clothes, or try factory and recycle shops

- use the library rather than buying books and magazines

- take advantage of free entertainment and recreational opportunities offered in your community.

There are so many things you can do to find $2 a day to put into tertiary education savings or your child's KiwiSaver fund. Find out more about KiwiSaver for children at www.nzkiwisaver.co.nz

Final Word

We all want to raise happy and successful children, but we often mistakenly think that money is the key to that happiness and success. In fact, the amount of money parents have makes very little difference to how their children turn out. The attitudes and actions of parents around money issues, though, have a huge effect.

On the positive side, parents who exhibit healthy money behaviours communicate strong values to their children. When parents talk openly and constructively about financial issues, avoid engaging in frequent money battles and use their financial resources to help the disadvantaged, children learn lessons about respect, love and giving.

On the negative side, unhealthy money behaviours can inadvertently distort the values parents want to communicate; they can also make their children very unhappy. Repeated fights about money may communicate to children that money isn't worth having because it's a source of anger, hostility, resentment and tension. When parents are workaholics who are rarely home, they communicate that making money and supporting an affluent lifestyle are more important than having meaningful family time.

Well, you've made it to the end and hopefully you are well on the way to graduating as a financially savvy parent. Such parents know how to emphasise the positive and minimise the negative. They understand that money in itself is neither good nor bad; it's what they do with it and what they teach their children about it that matter. Becoming this type of parent is a function of awareness and effort. You need to be aware of the beliefs and practices that define financially savvy parenting, as covered in this book, and then resolve to translate this awareness into action, thus helping your children to avoid becoming more victims of 'generation debt'.

Thank you for taking the time to help create a generation of financially literate adults.

Family activity idea

Learning about money

Learning about money is like a game we all play. There are actions that help children learn. The game on the next page will give you some ideas.

Go . . . To the store. Let the child see you exchange money for goods →	**Give** the child a coin to make a choice at a store	**Have** a bank and save coins	**Allowances** help set goals
Understand and plan for use of pay received			**Teach** a child to: • Save some • Share some • Spend some • Grow some
Learn to use credit	**Money-all-play** Parents have an important part in helping children learn about money management. They set examples, provide learning opportunities, and help children practise decision-making.		**Take a trip** Go to job sites with a parent or friend to see how money is earned
Get an education			**Set** goals
Set priorities based on needs versus wants			**Make** shopping lists **Look** at choices in catalogues and shopper ads
Learn to earn with extra tasks at home or outside the home	**Learn** to judge quality	**Plan** for a toy, gift or other purchase **Set** a budget	**Find . . .** low cost and free fun

Jargon busters

A money dictionary for children

What does 'budget' mean? What about 'debt' or 'in the black'? This money dictionary will help you to answer these questions using straightforward language.

Account You can have an account with a bank, building society or a Credit Union.

Advertisements (also called 'ads' or 'commercials' when on TV) The people who make things use ads to tell us how good those things are and why we should buy them. Ads can be on posters, in magazines and papers. We see a lot of them on TV.

Asset A valuable item that you own, such as a house, car, money in savings or in the share market.

ATM Automatic teller machine. This is a machine with a keypad and screen, which allows you to withdraw and deposit money using a plastic ATM card linked to your account.

Balance The amount of money in an account, equal to the amount coming in minus the amount being paid out.

Bank This is where many people keep their money. When they earn money it is put in the bank. People take it out of the bank when they need some money.

Banks will let people borrow money, but you have to pay extra. Banks will give you more money if you save in special accounts.

Bankrupt Sometimes people spend all the money they have so that they have none left. This happens to shops, factories and other businesses. They have to tell everyone they are bankrupt so that they can be helped to begin to sell the business and pay back some of the money they owe.

Bargain If you buy a bargain it means you spent less than the normal price! Sometimes a bargain can be where you get two things for the price of one.

Benefit The government will give money to people who cannot work, or who need help. This is called a benefit. Parents may be able to get a child benefit to help pay for some of the things you need.

Bet When you bet on something you give some money in the hope you will get more back. If the thing you bet on does not win you may lose all your money. Some people bet on whether their favourite sports team will win.

Bill People send you a bill when you need to pay for something, for example the electricity or water that we use at home.

Borrow To borrow money means that someone else lends you the money and you agree to pay them back as soon as possible.

Borrower   A borrower is someone who borrows money from someone else, or from a bank, building society, or loan company.

Budget   A budget is where you plan how you are going to spend the money that you have. Even the government does this!

Building society   A building society is now similar to a bank. They used to be places where people borrowed money to buy their houses.

Cash   Paper money and coins.

Charity   An organisation that works toward helping a certain cause or group of disadvantaged people.

Cheque   If you have an account you often get a cheque book. You write a cheque instead of paying with cash. The cheque tells the bank, building society or credit union how much money to take out of your account to pay for your goods.

Coin   Coins are made out of metal. They represent different amounts of money. Coins have been used for thousands of years. The Ancient Romans used coins.

Consumer   Someone who buys something from a shop.

Cost   The cost of something describes how much you have to pay to buy it.

Credit card A credit card lets people spend money without having to pay immediately. It's a form of borrowing; you have to pay it back at the end of the month or the credit card company will charge you extra money.

Credit union A credit union is similar to a bank but is owned and controlled by its members. You can borrow money, or just have a savings account with great interest rates and low fees.

Customer When you buy something, you are a customer.

Debit card This is like a cross between a credit card and a cheque. A debit card can be used to purchase goods and services. But unlike a credit card, the money comes directly out of your cheque account.

Debt If you owe people money, you are in debt to them.

Donate To offer your money or time to help a worthy cause.

Earn You earn money when you work, whether it be for a parent or a boss. Your boss pays you when you've done some work. She may pay you at the end of the week, or the end of the month.

Expenses Goods and services you pay money for.

Gamble A gamble is when someone bets on something in the hope they will win more money.

Goal   Something you want to achieve.

Goods   The things you buy are called goods.

In the black   This means you have money in your account.

In the red   You have insufficient funds in your account.

Income   This is the money you earn.

Income support   The government gives some people money to help them. Many people are allowed to claim this money, which is called income support. People have to fill in special forms.

Insurance   If you insure something it means you pay the insurance company money each month or year. If you have car insurance (compulsory in Australia but not in New Zealand) and have an accident the money you have paid helps to pay for the cost of repairs to the car. If the accident is your fault your insurance helps to pay for the other person's car as well. You may also have life insurance so that your debts are paid off and your family is looked after if you die.

Interest   If you save money in special accounts and don't spend it for a long time, you will earn extra money. This is called interest. The banks, building societies and credit unions pay you because you've let them have the use of your money while they look after it. They invest it and make more money and give you some of that!

Investment An investment may give you more interest than banks, building societies and credit unions. If you invest in something, you give your money for a long time. Sometimes you get more money, but with a poor investment you may lose all your money.

KiwiSaver A work-based retirement savings scheme, which is voluntary to join but compulsory for employers to facilitate.

Lender A lender is a person who lets others borrow money.

Loan Money temporarily given by a bank, person or business. Interest is usually paid on the loan, and the money must be paid back.

Long-term goal Something more expensive that you want to save for so that you can pay for it in the future, such as university education or a car.

Lottery The lottery is a gamble. People pay to see if their numbers will win. A few people win lots of money. Most people win no money at all.

Mortgage People use a mortgage to buy a house. A bank, building society or credit union lends them money. It's paid back every month over many years. People also pay interest on this money.

Note A note is a larger sum of money than coins (for example, $5, $10, $20, $50 and $100 notes).

Online shopping Nowadays many people shop using the internet. This is called online shopping. Supermarkets let you shop online and will deliver the goods to your door, but you pay extra for this service.

Owe If you owe money it means you've borrowed from someone and need to pay it back.

P & P This stands for postage and packing. If you have something sent to your house you often have to pay extra for the postage and for the people to pack the goods in a parcel.

Poverty This is where people have very little money and cannot buy many things. The government will help those who are living in poverty.

Price Everything you buy has a price. This is how much money you have to give to buy it.

Retirement plan When you start to earn money it's a good idea to begin to save a little money each month in a retirement scheme. When you stop working you will be given some of this money every week or month. The government takes some of your money every month to pay for state superannuation.

Risk This is a chance you take when you invest. You are taking a risk because you could lose money.

Save If you save your money you are able to buy things you want. It's good to save – for things that cost a lot, and in case you need to buy something in a hurry. Many people say they are 'saving for a rainy day'. This means if something happens and they can't earn money, they have some available when it's needed.

Secure site If you shop on the internet it's important to make sure you use a secure site so that no one knows your banking or credit card details. A picture of a lock should appear on the screen.

Share This is a piece of a company. You own shares of a company when you buy stock in it.

Shopper Anyone who buys something is a shopper.

Spend When you buy something, you have to hand over your money and you will have your purchase instead. It's always good to stop and think before you spend your money!

Spending power People who sell things are interested in your spending power. They hope you'll spend all your money buying their goods or services.

Statement Banks, building societies and credit unions send you a notice every month, or when you ask for it. These days you may only receive it online. This tells you how much money you still have in your account and lists the amounts you've spent. This is called a statement.

Tax Everyone who earns money has to pay tax to the government. This is so the government can pay for schools, hospitals and other services. You give some of your money so that everyone can have these things.

Wage When you work for someone, they pay you every week or month. This is called your wages (or salary). It's the money you earn by working.

Withdraw To take money out of an account.

Useful websites

For parents, teachers and children

This list of websites offers a wide range of great online resources to provide additional information about teaching children money skills.

General sites

www.practicalmoneyskills.com

PracticalMoneySkills.com is a website designed to help educators, parents and students practise better money management for life.

www.understandingmoney.gov.au This website was created by the Financial Literacy Foundation, which was established by the Australian government to give all Australians the opportunity to increase their financial knowledge and better manage their money.

www.allmoneymatters.com.au All Money Matters provides access to free money management resources and teaching products which help children to develop awareness of their money habits, attitudes and beliefs.

www.escapefromknab.com You are about to take off on an adventure to the strange and slimy planet of KNAB. Make the right choices while you are there and you can return to the planet Earth. Live dangerously and who knows what may happen. Good Luck!

www.orangechildren.com Discover Planet Orange, and open your eyes to the world of money! Brave the desert, climb mountains and dodge alligators while you explore everything there is to know about earning, spending, saving, and investing.

www.fpa.asn.au The Financial Planning Association of Australia Limited (FPA) is recognised internationally as the professional organisation representing the financial planning sector in Australia.

www.dollarsandsense.com.au This site provides a vast range of teaching resources for students between the ages of 14 and 18.

www.kidsmoney.com.au KIDS MONEY provides access to financial literacy resources following the guidelines established by the Australian government's Financial Literacy Taskforce. It is for parents to use with children aged five to 12.

www.enzt.co.nz The Young Enterprise Trust is a not-for-profit organisation helping to promote enterprise and financial literacy among the young. This site provides information on financial literacy programmes available in New Zealand schools.

www.sorted.org.nz Sorted is New Zealand's free, independent money guide, run by the Retirement Commission. It's full of calculators and information to help you manage your personal finances throughout life.

www.nzkiwisaver.co.nz A great site which answers frequently asked questions about KiwiSaver for employees, employers, self-employed, non-employees and children.

www.camelotgroup.co.nz Some of New Zealand's most experienced practitioners in the financial advisory industry, who are dedicated to providing first-class independent financial advice, have formed the Camelot Group. Camelot has a great website with many calculators.

www.ifa.org.nz The Institute of Financial Advisers, the professional body for financial planners, insurance advisers and investment advisers. The Institute is an industry leader, representing over 1400 financial advisers throughout New Zealand.

Saving sites

www.kidscashmanagement.com CHILDRENCA$H™, the Cash Management Workbook for Children.

www.themoneycamp.com Summer camps for children that make learning about how money works fun and easy to understand.

www.dailyfinances.co.uk Daily Finances contains over 70 articles written by experts who continually update and add new content.

Spending sites

www.kidsmoney.org Chock-a-block full of resources for parents and children.

www.younginvestor.com A cool website where you can get the scoop on investing or just have fun playing money games.

www.jumpstart.org Jump$tart Coalition for Personal Financial Literacy promotes teaching of personal finance to young adults.

www.independentmeans.com The leading provider of products and services for girls' financial independence, and for parents trying to raise financially fit children.

www.bankrate.com Comprehensive, objective, free information on credit cards, mortgages, auto loans, university financing and more.

Sharing sites

www.foundationburma.org The Foundation for the People of Burma (FPB). FPB has been delivering humanitarian aid to people in Burma and refugees along its borders for a decade. FPB has extensive project partnerships that enable it to broaden its effectiveness without garnering too much attention – something that matters in Burma.

www.giraffe.org The nonprofit Giraffe Heroes Project fosters active citizenship by telling the stories of

'Giraffes' (real heroes, people who stick their necks out for the common good) in the media, on podiums and in the K-12 Giraffe Heroes Program.

www.justgive.org JustGive is a non-profit organisation whose mission is to connect people with the charities and causes they care about and to increase overall giving.

www.fdncenter.org Recognising the importance of involving youth in charitable activities in order to develop the next generation of philanthropists, The Foundation Centre provides this useful resource list for people interested in encouraging youth philanthropy and voluntarism.

Bibliography

Crary, E., *Pick up your socks,* Parenting Press, Seattle, 1990.

Danes, S.M., 'Money, children, and allowances', *Young Families Newsletter,* 100, Minnesota Extension Service, St. Paul, 1991.

Danes, S.M., 'Parental perceptions of children's financial socialization', in *Proceedings of the Association for Financial Counselling and Planning Education,* D.R. Iams (Ed.), Charleston, SC, 1992.

Danes, S.M., *Allowances and alternatives,* FO-6117, Minnesota Extension Service, St. Paul, 1992.

Felder, L., 'Moneywise children: Teach children early to save, earn, spend sensibly', *Parents,* 65(5), 1990.

Hogarth, J.M., Swanson, J. and Lino, M., *Children and money: An overview; How children get money Preschoolers and money; School age children and money; Money and teens,* Consumer Economy and Housing Topics, New York Cooperative Extension Service, 1983.

Miller, J. and Yung, S., 'The role of allowances in adolescent socialization', *Youth and Society,* 137–159, 1990.

Mills Morrow, A., 'Money management', Lesson 1 in *Money sense for your children,* Oregon State University Extension Service.

Money Management Institute. *Children and money management,* Money Management Institute, Prospect Heights, IL, 1981.

Schuchardt, J., Danes, S., Swanson, J. and Westbrook, E., 'Financial management literacy for American youth', in *37th Annual American Council on Consumer Interests Proceedings,* V. Hademann (Ed.), Columbia, MO, 1991.

Smith, G. and Parkow, D., *Money in our children's hands,* HE-247, North Dakota State University Extension Service, 1990.

Stipp, H.H., 'Children as consumers', *American Demographics,* 10(2), 27–32, 1988.

Waddell, F.E., *Money and your children,* Genesis Press, Baton Rouge, 1985.

Walker, R. and Hathaway, I., *Helping your child learn to manage money,* NCR392, Michigan Extension Service and North Central Region Publication, USDA, 1991.

About the author

Andrew Lendnal is a financial author and educator. For several years he has been directly involved in helping children learn about money, has advised financial institutions on how best to encourage children to save, and has given seminars and work shops on the subject. His first book, *Budget Wise, Dollar Rich* (with Anton Nadilo) was published by Exisle in 2005, and he has since written two books for children. He is employed by the Grosvenor Financial Services Group (who provide products and services for the Camelot Group), where he is Head of Marketing and Head of the Grosvenor KiwiSaver scheme. Andrew lives in Wellington and has one daughter.

The following websites provide more information on this book: www.goldstart.com.au or www.goldstart.co.nz.

Special piggy bank offer

The world's first inflatable piggy bank is available at a special price to purchasers of *Gold Start.* Suitable for young children, it is available in various colours from the author's website. Normally $12.99 (plus p&p), you can purchase it for just $4.99 (plus p & p).

Visit www.moneysavvydna.com and enter the special code.

Free membership of the Money Savvy DNA community

Money Savvy DNA helps you teach your children about money. Join now to receive the regular e-zine, *Money Strands Club for parents.* It has great ideas and techniques to help you teach your child about money. To join the community, visit the website: www.moneysavvydna.com and click on FREE membership.

Back Cover Material

Gold Start **is the book that millions of parents have been waiting for: a book that provides parents, teachers and caregivers with the necessary tools to teach children the four basic principles of money management – Earning, Spending, Saving and Sharing.**

- Do you have a plan to educate your children about financial matters?

- Are you uncomfortable talking about money with your children?

- Do you use money as a bribe to get your children to do things?

- Do you argue with your partner about money in front of your children?

- Do you give your children a consistent allowance?

- Are you worried about how your children will get through university?

Financial author and educator Andrew Lendnal has been directly involved in helping children learn about money for several years, and believes that teaching money basics at a very early age is crucial. In fifteen practical lessons, he outlines the skills that toddlers, preschoolers, school-aged children and tweens require to be money savvy, followed by a special section focusing on teens and money. Full of handy practical tips, *Gold Start* also includes many family activities and games that will help children learn about money in a fun way, making this book both a handbook and a catalyst for family discussions about finances.

Made in the USA
Middletown, DE
08 July 2025